The Complete Guide to Manifes

THE COMPLETE GUIDE TO
MANIFESTING *with* CRYSTALS

Marina Costelloe

Author of
The Complete Guide to Crystal Astrology

EARTHDANCER

A FINDHORN PRESS IMPRINT

Publisher's Note

All information in this book has been compiled according to the publisher's best knowledge and belief. People react in different ways however, and therefore neither the publisher nor the author can, for individual cases, provide a guarantee as to the effectiveness or harmlessness of the applications described herein. In cases of serious physical or mental health concerns, please consult a physician, alternative practitioner, or psychologist.

First edition 2009

Marina Costelloe
The Complete Guide to Manifesting with Crystals

Copyright © Earthdancer GmbH 2009
Text Copyright © Marina Costelloe 2009

First published in UK in 2009 by Earthdancer GmbH an imprint of:
Findhorn Press, 305a The Park, Findhorn, Forres IV36 3TE, Great Britain

Cover design: Dragon Design UK Ltd.
Cover photography: Manifestation Crystal © Manfred Feig; Sun and water © ANP/Shutterstock;
    Hands © Juriah Mosin/Shutterstock
Editing: Claudine Eleanor Bloomfield

Typesetting by Dragon Design UK Ltd.
Typeset in ITC Garamond condensed

Printed in China – 100% of the paper used for this book is sourced from responsibly managed forests

ISBN 978-1-84409-169-0

This book is dedicated to world peace

Contents

Introduction

Energize your being
Focus your spirit
Attract the things you want
Manifest positive outcomes in your life

Have you noticed that there are people in our world who live an enchanted life? They seem to manifest the things they want and need as easily as they draw breath. This is so because such people live in complete harmony with their wishes, goals and values, and they have confidence. Manifesting is easy to them. Move into that enchanted space, understand your wishes, goals and values, and you too will see that life becomes crystal clear.

You can create the reality you desire. You can conceive, visualize, and manifest it. *The Complete Guide to Manifesting with Crystals* will map a path for you to move forward with confidence in your life. This book shows how positive action, focused intention, crystal energy and timing attract the things you need, want, hope for and expect. Crystal energy combined with positive action can change lives. There is tremendous power in prayer and positive thought. Crystals support our highest purpose, help realign our intentions, and focus our desires.

A need or desire is not always to do with an object; maybe it is a loving relationship you need in your life, or happiness, peace, joy, or balance. It comes as a surprise to many people that the secret recipe for happiness is to align your time, energy and wishes with your higher self's life plan. Crystal energy places you at the crossroads of time, energy, your wishes and your higher self's plan so that you can manifest a new reality.

The word 'manifesting' in *Manifesting with Crystals* means creating an observable change in your life, according to your own design. Keep reading to find out how to direct change and amplify positive outcomes in your life. Do you currently practice positive affirmations, positive speech, manifesting mantras, and/or use creative picture boards? If so, have you seen an observable change in your situation as a result? If your answer is 'Yes', then fantastic! You have the mindset to make things happen. But if, like so many of us, you feel as though something is missing in your manifesting – that extra energy, motivation, readily observable outcomes, or even a place to begin – it may be that you need to add a bit of crystal energy to your life.

If you are new to crystals, there are many ways to introduce crystal energy into your life. A garden stone, a large quartz crystal, a river pebble, a diamond ring – all of these are gifts from the earth and can support a loving change in your life. In *Manifesting with Crystals*, the term 'crystal' may refer to minerals, gems, metals, elements from the periodic table, rocks and stones. This is consistent with the way 'crystal' is defined in most if not all New Age books (including those written by Gienger, Hall and Melody), and embraces natural crystals, rocks, stones, shells, opals, amber, minerals, periodic table elements, gemstones, metals, synthetic (man-made) or enhanced crystals, gemstones, and refined metals. Look around at your world; the beauty in it belongs to you. Open your eyes to the wonder in every rock, stone and crystal, knowing that it was divine timing that brought it to your awareness. You already have crystal friends helping you!

Crystals can help you identify and stay true to your life path by connecting you with your higher purpose. This book will help you identify the best crystals to support your life path. Choosing the best crystals for you at the right time feels great; its like finding a new best friend. If you are new to crystals, keep an eye out for the 'Crystal Hints' in each chapter – they will give you a useful crystal working list to use until you find your own crystal buddies.

The most fulfilling path through life is achieved by vibrating in harmony with all thoughts (energy) and things (matter). You are connected to all energy and matter, and therefore to the universal consciousness, and realizing this can help you gain control of your life path and reach your full potential. Your ability to manifest positive outcomes will occur in your life when you are 'in sync' with the universal consciousness. Crystal Synchronization is the act of using crystals to get 'in sync' with your divine purpose. Timing is everything. Crystal Synchronization is the active ingredient in being able to ask for the right thing at the right time. It works by attracting to you the objects and events that are karmically on your horizon, in a way that will support your circumstances. When you can minimize challenges and enhance positive outcomes by using crystal manifesting techniques, confidence builds and more blessings become real.

Before embarking on this path, look within yourself. Consider the consequences of your activities, and take responsibility for your actions and motivations. You may not always receive exactly what you desire, when you desire it. In times of pain and fear you may feel needy and demand that the Universe provide you with any number of things in a short timeframe; don't be surprised when these demands do not manifest in the way you had wished. Re-centre yourself in love and hope, and see the blessing in the challenge. Try not to be fearful; look towards a full life, filled with endless opportunities. A perfect life is not for this world or our lifetime. A faultless, flawless life is frozen and sterile and not something on which to be wasting your positive intentions.

Manifesting with Crystals gives real-life examples of how to manifest positivity in your life through living a fruitful partnership with crystal energy. Many crystal energizing techniques are provided, including the use of crystals with mantras, candles, water, music, aromatherapy, massage and meditation. As each crystal works differently with each individual, *Manifesting with Crystals* focuses on a variety of techniques to use with the crystals *you* love.

Many crystals are talked about and referred to in *Manifesting with Crystals* and I would like to say straight away that it is by no means necessary to try and obtain every crystal in its physical form; there is great benefit to be gained in simply looking at a picture, or touching a stone in a natural environment or museum. As you read on, you may well find that several crystals resonate with you, and it is my firm belief that the best crystal for you will come your way if you are meant to work with it in the physical plane. Magic happens - if you are aware and in need of a crystal, it will find its way to you.

Manifesting positivity means that real and positive change observably happens in your life. 'Banking positivity' is a new term discussed in detail in *Manifesting with Crystals*, and is a 'how to' technique to save and store positive energy so that in times of desperation, sadness or confusion you can draw on these reserves. Its key lies in your own daily life experience, your family, and your karmic connections, and will therefore be different for every individual. The easiest way to manifest what you want is to make positive choices, to bank positivity.

Read on to discover a useable framework to raise intention energy, recognize divine love, and to realize your full potential and positive life path. Manifest a heart–soul energy awareness and the rest will take care of itself. Use this book as a personal evolution guide for awareness, happiness, love and prosperity. My hope is that you will look at crystals in a new light, discover how each is important in your life, and then use them to energize yourself while keeping true to who you are. Remember you can tap into crystal energy to focus your intentions, manifest your goals, support your soul journey and attract abundance into your life.

I love crystals and suspect you do too. Remember you are as unique and beautiful as the energy that is in each and every crystal. With eternal perspective both the diamond and the river pebble have magical potential and a divine purpose. Please remember that crystal energy and universal energy are interconnected – use your crystal connections wisely, with love and compassion, in all ways, for the good of all. The focus in *Manifesting with Crystals* is a positive one – look to the energy in crystals to support you in your personal ascension process.

Attraction and Amplification Using Crystals

The Law of Attraction and the 'High Five'

The Law of Attraction is a popular concept which maintains that your thoughts, conscious and unconscious, create your reality. Many wonderful books and films delve into this amazing concept much further than *Manifesting with Crystals*; here the focus is on how crystals increase positive outcomes associated with the Law of Attraction. Quite simply, crystal energy amplifies the process of manifesting. Crystals amplify the law of attraction. Crystals are a bridge between thoughts, events and material things. Crystal energy can support you in your quest to live a happy and fulfilling life, and help you gain control of your life path.

Manifesting requires truth, spirit and love to create a new reality. Manifesting happens when the following occur in the same time and space, thereby bringing about positive change:

Positive Feeling

Positive Thought

Positive Action

Positive Will

Positive Energy

I call these the *High Five*. Crystal energy supports and amplifies the High Five.

Universal creative forces are contained in the High Five. Earth, Air, Fire, Water and Spirit are the elements that create and sustain life, growth and change.

Feelings = Water
To manifest something, you really need to be connected emotionally to it, in the present moment.

Thoughts = Air
Positive thoughts and all forms of communication need to clearly state what it is you want to manifest.

Actions = Earth
Positive action involves analysis, planning, and diligent effort to expediate success.

Will = Fire
Move toward your goal with confidence, generosity and enthusiasm.

Energy = Spirit
A soul filled with love finds anything possible.

Combine what you already know about the Law of Attraction and use crystals to create your new reality.

A Manifesting Quartz Crystal

There is a particular crystal that embodies all that is the Law of Attraction – a Manifesting Quartz Crystal. Isabel Silveira writes in her beautiful book *Quartz Crystals,* 'A manifesting crystal is characterized as a larger crystal with a small crystal totally contained within it'. A manifesting crystal 'carries the knowledge of how we can manifest our dreams, desires and objectives in our material reality.'[1] These crystals can occur inside natural points, or may be fashioned into a shape such as a sphere, egg or generator; sizes range from less than one centimeter right up to giant crystals over one meter long. Quartz is very potent, and holds many properties including the concentrating of insight, intuition, healing and divination; most importantly it brings into reality that which we thought was only in potential. Manifesting quartz crystals are a visual reminder that all we need to fulfill our destiny is already contained within us. As we look upon the crystal within the crystal, we see our inner dreams and their manifestation in the physical world. These crystals hold abundant energy, which, when combined with our High Five, brings about positive change in our world. If you are blessed to own or receive a Manifesting Quartz Crystal, you will be able to use it in any of the techniques described in *Manifesting with Crystals*. If you do not own or have access to a Manifesting Quartz Crystal, the chapter entitled 'Choosing the Right Crystal for You' will guide you in how to find the perfect crystal to enhance your manifesting abilities.

Positive affirmations, manifesting mantras, positive communication, and creative visualization picture boards are all techniques associated with the Law of Attraction, and they can bring about observable changes in your life. If you have tried them before today, you will already know!

Positive Affirmations Using Crystals

A positive affirmation is a sequence of words to help connect the mind, body and spirit with one focus. For example:

Affirmation: MY FAMILY IS PROSPEROUS.

Affirmations used like a mantra - repeated over and over - can sustain positive outcomes in meditation, manifesting, earth healing, protection, acceptance and surrender. Thoughtful, positive affirmations can change lives; there is great power in them. Affirmations become even more powerful when they hold positive intentions for the greater good and benefit the collective.

Repetition is very important: repeat your chosen affirmation often - in words, thoughts, writing, singing and art - with a happy and grateful heart. Increase the potency of your affirmation by holding a favorite crystal in your hand while saying it. The crystal you are holding is gently supporting and amplifying your thought patterns.

Crystal Hint for Positive Affirmations: Garnet, Gold, Tiger Eye, Rose Quartz, Agate. These crystals sustain energy flow into your solarplexus and heart chakra, maintaining self confidence during your affirmation sessions.

Positive Communication Using Crystals

Positive speech is a powerful tool; it is akin to being environmentally responsible for your communication. There is no doubt about it, negative communication is polluting, wastes time, and takes a lot of effort to clean up. Positive communication is enjoyable and promotes growth, diversity and sustainability. Listen to your words carefully and choose to share words of support, love, encouragement and understanding. Remove gossip, blame, fear and resentment from your life by changing the dialogue your mind creates. By clarifying your words your energy increases, your confidence grows, and great things start to happen. Start introducing terms like 'I can...', 'I will...', 'We deserve...' and 'Let's negotiate...'. These build up an aura of self control, balance and light. Listen to your thoughts; consider the internal dialogue that is going on while you are living your life - brushing your teeth, waiting in a queue, falling asleep, eating your meals. Check in with your thoughts often. Keep in mind that gossip and hurtful words waste a lot of energy, drag down potential, and keep us in a place we do not want to be. Keep small tumbled stones in your pocket or wallet to support you in your quest for positive communication change.

Crystal Hint for Positive Communication: Rhodonite, Selenite, Clear Quartz, Tourmaline. These crystals promote individuality while connecting you safely to the environment around you. Clear Quartz in particular dispels self illusion, silencing your inner critic. Take these stones out of your pocket and hold them in your hand when you find yourself in need of extra support.

Creative Visualisation Using Crystals

Creative visualisation is a fun way to keep your true desires, hopes and dreams in sight. Find a place in your home where you pass by frequently, and start a collection of things you desire; you could include pictures, words, toys, scale replicas, postcards, books, etc. You may choose to collect cards with beautiful motivational sayings like 'treat yourself', or single words such as 'hope', 'love' and 'grace' written on lovely paper. Photos of you and your family in happy times, a picture of a healthy planet, a list of things you want to do - all these things can help remind you of your dreams. Keep treasures received from loved ones in this creative visualisation area, praying for their continued happiness and safety. When passing your collection, feel happiness and gratitude for the things you desire. Imagine how it would be if they were in your life, and be grateful for these things as if they have already manifested for you. Keep some of your most beloved crystals in this place to attract your attention and channel your focus to your highest ideals.

> **Crystal Hint for creative visualisation:** Citrine for better finances, Rose Quartz for love, and Amethyst for the transmutation of successful ideas and actions into our space and time. These crystals are tools that amplify your thoughts, focus your strength and power, and light up your future.

As you manifest something from your creative visualisation space, remove the item or picture that represented it and put an offer of gratitude in its place - maybe a charity donation receipt, a thank you note, a prayer of thanks, or a promise to do a good deed to help someone else.

The Four Most Common Blocks to Manifesting

Sometimes there is something we particularly desire that may not come swiflty or in the form we want. Why does this happen? There are four common blocks to manifesting: a lack of gratitude, a closed mind, a judgemental attitude, and drama. Thankfully, once these blocks are understood, there are ways to work with and dissolve these barriers to your success.

Lack of Gratitude corresponds with ignorance and resentment, it limits the exchange of good will. Gratitude is a life-changing gift to your self. People who show appreciation and give thanks have happier lives, feel in control of their future, and generally cope with life with grace and ease.

When you manifest some change in your life for the better, express gratitude - real, heartfelt gratitude. Feel the sensation of thankfulness; it is wonderful. You can advance the practice of gratitude by incorporating a form of practical gratitude known as 'pay it forward' - usually a missing element in manifesting guides. 'Pay it forward' is a simple way of sharing the abundance you have in your life; you simply repay abundance by giving. It is no longer sustainable to believe that we can each live in an individual world that has no interaction or impact on anyone or anything else. Practical gratitude – the act of giving thanks in a practical way – strenghtens our connectivity with the world, opens new opportunities, and increases the flow of universal energy into our lives. Remember that the power of attraction is heightened when visualizing things for the collective good.

Practical gratitude amplifies your success in manifesting; it is that simple. Understanding and adopting practical gratitude removes blocks to sucessful manifesting. Please be mindful that gratitude isn't a tool you can use to bargain your way into or out of something you are trying to manifest. Sincere and joyful gratitude is crucial in manifesting positive outcomes.

> **Crystal Hint for gratitude:** White Howlite or Carnelian to express gratitude for the abundant goodness in you life.

A closed mind implies a lack of awareness that insulates us from the reality of the present and the possibility of the future. A closed mind is like a huge wall preventing any view of the future from entering your awareness. Fear, exhaustion, sadness, pain and regret often stand in our way, creating thought processes that stand in the way of success. To move beyond this block, be kind and understanding to yourself and accept that all emotions are transient.

> **Crystal Hint for an open mind:** Alexandrite to open your mind to new opportunities.

A judgmental attitude often goes along with having a closed mind, and is like looking at your future through a tiny hole; you only get to see the bit you allow yourself to see. Unconditional love provides the freedom to explore and create new realities. A mind that is open and willing to consider new ideas is a mind not constrained to the space it occupies; cultivating an open mind and attitude is a big step in successful manifesting.

> **Crystal Hint for an open attitude:** Kunzite to promote unconditional love, kindness, and intuitive awakening.

Drama is created when people blow things out of proportion, blame others and impose self-limiting choices. 'Drama queens' use phrases like: 'I don't have...', 'I can't do that...', 'They will think I am...', 'You won't believe what happened to me...', 'Why does it always happen to me?', 'Why don't they help me?', 'I'll never get...', each with the undercurrent of not taking any responsibility for self-action. Drama dialogue disconnects the 'drama queen' from their life path. Hurting and despondent, these people create a drama cycle that is difficult to stop.

> **Crystal Hint to dispel drama:** Charoite enhances truthful self-expression as an avenue for change.

All blocks scatter your precious energy, the very same energy that could have been used for manifesting. Of course there will be ups and downs in life, but if you can proceed with confidence, light and love, and build on those feelings every day, you will suceed. Make your life a spiritual journey and manifest the best into your life – you **can** do it. Confidence and gratitude support a manifesting mind state. All crystals, and metals including Silver, Gold, Brass and Copper, support confidence and gratitude.

Our Universe is made of energy, light and matter; it vibrates and oscillates; everything within it is constantly moving, changing, reacting, absorbing and recycling. Crystals are an active facilitator between matter and energy. As in nature, our lives can change so fast. Greatness, fame or fortune can come and go in the blink of an eye, but beauty beyond belief can stay in our memories forever. In so many different ways life tests our resolve to be true to the self. Never underestimate your ability to change your life. Change is only a moment away. Be prepared and confident for life's challenges, and you will succeed.

Crystal Synchronization

What Is It?

In ancient cities – Atlantis, Lemuria, Egypt, Machu Picchu (the Crystal City) and the cities of many other empires – crystals, gems, rocks and stones were fundamental to living in total awareness. Great civilizations, ancient and modern, hold crystals in high regard, utilizing them in religious services, garments, crowns, sceptres, orbs, swords, and rings, as personal adornment and to signify and amplify spiritual power. The continued attraction to crystals over thousands of years is no coincidence. Crystals are timeless entities with enormous energy stores. Crystal workers tap into the genesis energy contained in crystals and can help you work with crystals in your life. Many crystal workers are blessed with the intuition to read crystal energy, and are able to prescribe the right crystal for you and your healing needs. Crystal Synchronization is essentially the same thing but for manifesting, finding the right energy to move you into the right place at the right time. Crystal Synchronization is the act of realigning your life using crystals.

Crystal Synchronization brings together (synchronizes) the best time, best energy and best wishes in order to manifest happy changes in your life. Crystal Synchronization raises your awareness so that you can ask for the right thing at the right time. When you enhance your perception and open your eyes and heart, you receive. When you are open to receiving, you can attract, accelerate, strengthen, motivate, and complete your goals. You can be 'in sync' with your divine purpose; you can change your life.

Have a quick look around your home, what crystals do you already have access to? Inside the house you may have precious and semi precious jewellry, Silver, Brass, Gold, Glass, Magnets. Outside your home there are Pebbles, garden Rocks, Shells and other natural beauties. If you find you don't have access to an assortment of crystals, find images from books, the Internet and New Age magazines, and place the pictures in your creative visualization area. Crystal energy knows no time or space and with awareness you can connect to an individual crystal energy vibration as easily as you connect to a particular colour. Take some time to learn about the crystals you have found, spend time with them and notice how they change. When purchasing crystals remember some may be colour enhanced to improve their appeal. In my personal experience colour enhancement does not alter the innate properties of the crystal as far as manifesting goes. Colour enhancement boosts a crystal's potency in colour therapy, aura integration and chakra balancing in some people, and not in others. The most important thing is to be completely aware of the crystals you own or purchase – find out if a crystal is natural, enhanced in some way, or man-made. You will soon see how crystals work in your life. I know some crystal workers who only work with natural crystals and others who work with success using with a wide variety of enhanced, man-made, natural, and/or polished crystals.

How to Synchronize

Crystal Synchronization allows hopes, desires and dreams to have the greatest potential of being realized. Getting our High Five 'in sync' – positive Feeling, Thought, Action, Will and Energy – requires some effort. First, select a crystal to work with from your collection, a crystal that feels light to the touch.

> **Crystal Hint for Crystal Synchronization:** Clear Quartz Crystal (manifesting, channeling, sphere, transmitting or window form).

Sit comfortably and write or think about appropriate ways to successfully fulfill your goals. This need only take a few minutes. Pay close attention to the first things that pop into your head; it is important to process all feelings at this stage. Don't judge your thoughts; let them all run their course. Now plan a strategy that includes creative visualization with crystal energy, and plan activities that will bring you closer to your goals. Enjoy the experience, feel confident in your plans and expect positive outcomes. Centre yourself in love and see all the pieces of the puzzle coming together.

When your High Five are 'in sync' with your divine purpose, change will happen. Crystal Synchronization attracts objects and events that are karmically available in a reasonable time frame. By focusing manifesting energy toward the best thing for you, your wish has a greater chance of being realized. Crystal Synchronization helps you steer clear of challenges, which in turn builds confidence and directly leads to successful manifesting. You will know when you are not on your path – obstacles stand in your way; you don't have energy to compelete the most basic tasks; there seems to be no light at the end of the tunnel. Movement in the form of positive action is the motivator for change. Change one thing and allow the Universe to help you find your way back to your path.

Crystal Synchronization shifts your current energy state to one that moves you straight forward to your goal. The speed of change is proportional to the input you provide. All change and growth is an interaction of energy. When your higher self and your destiny merge together, life becomes enchanted. When you are aware, positive, and headed in the right direction (your life path), external influences will still reach you, but you have a clear path and can move along faster, suffering less and gaining more.

Awareness of your situation creates choice; how to proceed becomes clearer, and your life path, though hidden, becomes clearer and clearer. Choose to change your life sooner rather than later.

Why Does This Crystal Make Me Feel So ... ?

Crystals motivate change; rarely do crystals have zero impact on a person. When working with crystals you will experience many different sensations, and, if you intend to work with crystals in the long term, it is a good idea to create a crystal diary, even if you have a good memory. Just like friends, not everyone fits perfectly. Some of the less pleasant feelings from crystal work can include; nausea, poor memory, itching, seemingly poor luck, irrational judgment, breakages (breakdowns). Usually these things happen when the crystal is out of sync with your current situation, and, more permanently, with your life path. Just as Crystal Synchronization can help you on your path, when you and your crystal are not in tune life can seem off-centre.

Before you condemn or banish a crystal, consider first what your day has been like. If you feel clear that it is the crystal affecting you, ask yourself some questions:

What are the exact feelings associated with this crystal?

Is it just this crystal or all crystals by this name?

Is it a mixed feeling or is it a distinct feeling?

At times even the negative feelings we experience around crystals are healing, learning lessons. Crystals help us interact creatively with the material world. There are many practical reasons a crystal feels uncomfortable to you, for example:

✧ Preconceived ideas regarding aspects like colour enhancement may directly influence you.

✧ You may have conscious or unconscious (past life) memories associated with the crystal.

✧ You may have physical allergies, particularly to metals.

✧ You may have an aversion to the crystal's perceived colour, which changes as your aura changes.

✧ Your energy vibration may not be resonating on a harmonious frequency.

✧ Your crystal astrology may have a difficult aspect involving this crystal.

✧ This crystal may be meant for you but for a different time.

If you are sure this crystal is not supporting you at this time, and it is not helping you learn an important lesson, you might choose to to do one (or more) of the following:

✧ Cleanse the crystal with incense, other crystals, sunlight or moonlight (suggested reading: *Purifying Crystals* by Michael Gienger). This may help you re-connect to the crystal and/or re-energize your crystal.

✧ Place the crystal in a quiet place and wait for the timing to change. It is particularly helpful if you can put the crystal behind glass with a buffer between you and the crystal.

✧ Keep moving the crystal around your home until you find it a happy position – some crystals need a bit of distance from people to do their thing.

✧ Pass the crystal on to a new owner. The crystal may have landed in your path for the sole purpose of being passed on in gratitude to someone who can really utilize and love it.

✧ If you are absolutely certain this is not a positive crystal in any time or place, you may consider burying it in a public park; this kind of neutral ground can help release your connection to the crystal. Whether in a park or elsewhere, you are returning the crystal to the earth element. Leave the crystal there to be cleansed by the earth. Do not return to collect it; you have released it from your life.

If you have a less than pleasant reaction to a crystal, don't force your lesson or experience on other people; a crystal may not work for you but may be valued or needed by someone close to you. Once a judgment has been made by you about a difficult crystal, it will take some undoing for the block to be released. Keep in mind that the law of attraction works well when we engage in positive communication. Make a small note describing the crystal by name and stating that the crystal has been 'released to do its work elsewhere'. Pearls are a good example of powerful manifestors that somehow got a poor reputation. Pearls have been reputed to be bad luck, which is just not true. Of course not everyone will resonate beautifully with these splendid gems of the sea, but if you are looking to enhance beauty, creativity, or to become pregnant, a pearl may be just the ticket. Fresh-water pearls accentuate natural charm and artistic talent, particularly in women. Ocean pearls help realize an individual's true potential and, if worn during a wedding ceremony, the true potential of the relationship.

Crystal Hint for boundaries: Smoky Quartz and Chiastolite both support safe boundary setting and offer spiritual protection.

Release

Release is as important as attracting a good job, a fine car and money for the bills. Until we release the energy ties that are holding us back we cannot fulfill our true potential. This is a lifelong series of 'spring cleanings of the soul', but practice makes perfect. Consider this: you are a free being, but you may be tied down by negative thoughts, gossip, poor choices or difficult situations. These things drag you down, steal your energy and make your future appear dim. Why do we hold on to so many terrible things? Often because we are fearful of the emptiness, the space that remains once we let go. As you release pain and sadness you will feel empowered, your self confidence will grow and your personal power will be restored. Releasing each bind will open more space for new opportunities. Release is not forgetting; to release is to not hold on anymore. The energy it takes to hold on can now be used to manifest positivity into your life.

Consider releasing:
◊ Negative feelings toward individuals
◊ Bitter memories
◊ Vindictive thoughts
◊ Envy
◊ Bad habits
◊ Ties to old projects, items, and behavior patterns
◊ Grief
◊ Guilt

Crystals to Support Healing Release
Yellow Calcite is best used for emotional release, resolving fears, and aiding integration into new situations. Working softly and gently, Yellow Calcite helps you heal your solarplexus. Yellow Calcite fills the void left when you let go, so you don't feel alone.

Iceland Spar (Clear Calcite) aids mental relaxation, emotional release and spiritual cleansing. Iceland Spar is best used for detoxing the body and releasing physical pain. Iceland Spar feels very liberating and exhilarating; it re-awakens the body to its true biorhythms once again.

Chrysocolla, the blue-green, copper-rich crystal, purifies and renews the self and the immediate environment, and releases pent-up emotions. Possibly the best crystal to heal medical stress.

Orange Aventurine fires up optimism; it frees up space so you feel lighthearted and refreshed, ready to give yourself a second (or third) chance.

The High Five for Release

Positive Feeling - Find somewhere you feel safe to sit, make yourself comfortable.
Positive Thought - Slow your internal dialogue and replace it with a new story.
Positive Action - Analyse how the past has affected the person you are today.
Positive Will - Be kind to yourself.
Positive Energy - Sit with a crystal to support release. Placed the crystal in your lap or next to you. Send yourself love, connect with universal love, and dissolve the ties you had to the past.

In the beginning the feelings will be intense; accept the situation knowing that what you have been through happened in the past. The suffering you have endured has surely made you a more aware and empathetic person, and that is a blessing. As you deal with your troubles you can help others resolve theirs. You may never know how a change in your actions, aura and thoughts looks to other people. Others mimic what they admire, and a shift in your energy, in your outlook, will have a ripple effect that gently touches kindred spirits. As gratitude and an open mind remove blocks to manifesting, so does release. By releasing you have dissolved another barrier to success.

> **Crystal Hint for releasing guilt**: Sodalite absolves past transgressions and promotes self forgiveness.

How to Choose the Right Crystals for You

You are unique and have a set of life experiences that makes you who you are. Your memories, hopes, dreams, wishes, pain and love are etched on your etheric aura. Do you need reminding how beautiful, strong and deserving you are? The very things that make you the wonderful person you are determine how you proceed with life, what happens next, and how you manifest with crystals. You will resonate differently with different crystal groups; some you will prefer, others not so much. In this chapter you will discover various ways to find the right crystal for you. Manifest the best crystals to support your life path.

Crystals... so many varieties, stunning colours, varying sizes and shapes ... an endless supply of individuality, energy and life. Be attentive to the crystals you already own; look with determination and purpose at these crystals for they have crossed your path for a reason. Take a moment to note their names, assess how they came into your life, and notice where you keep them. Which is currently your favourite and why? Open your mind to the opportunity that other supporting crystals will come into your life. Believe that your personal manifesting crystal is either already within your grasp or very close to you.

Crystals are grouped by common names and common attributes (Jasper, Quartz, Agate, etc.), but each is unique. We resonate with groups of crystals in our own paticular way. Some groups of crystals, for example the quartz group, support a wide range of people and uses. Clear Quartz holds many properties, including the connection to universal energy and the concentration of insight, intuition, healing and divination; and, as we have discovered, it makes the best general manifesting crystal. The more crystals you connect with, the more you will start to recognize their impact on you and how life changes when you are near them.

The crystals commonly considered to be 'essential' in a crystal kit are Clear Quartz, Rose Quartz, Smokey Quartz, Amethyst, Agate, Obsidian, Carnelian, Aventurine and Fluorite. These nine crystals form a workable base set for healing, manifesting, and crystal work. Surrounding yourself with one or many of these crystals is nourishing for the soul. It is not essential to have the biggest, best, most expensive crystal collection. Size and cost have no influence on the level of energy a crystal holds. Like most things in life, it's about balance; a balance of a few well-chosen crystals will help you feel connected to your higher self and the world around you.

It appears that enlightened souls who came here to tidy up family karma, raise the collective consciousness and help others learn about spirit have illness and physical challenges to work through too. This is a part of the light worker's path, and crystals can help. However, please seek professional medical advice from your doctor and other healthcare providers in regard to any current medical conditions, genetic dispositions, diagnoses and treatment options, as this book is not in any way a substitute for medical advice.

So how do you go about choosing the right crystal for you? What is your personal crystal? Which crystal supports you in finding your life path and sticking to it? Which crystal ignites the powerhouse inside you, motivating you to be the very best you can be? Which crystal helps you energize your personality, provides a spiritual mirror to your higher self, opens the doors to a new, bright self-image? Finding the right crystals for you is a deeply personal journey of discovery. A good place to begin is by finding your sacred stone, the stone that resonates with your essence and will lead you towards a magical life. You may already own your sacred stone; it may be in your favorite piece of jewellry, it may be the tumbled stone you have in your bag, or it may be just about to make itself known to you.

Birthstones

Let's begin by looking at some traditional and non traditional ways people have found their sacred stones. Traditional and modern birthstones support you by protecting you from harm, and bringing you good fortune. It is a long-held belief that a birthstone is the luckiest crystal to own, and that the power of your birthstone enhances your talents and energizes your life. There are a number of birthstone charts linking gemstones with calendar months or zodiac months. There are also ancient birthstone lists dating back over 1000 years for Arabic, Hebrew, Hindu and Roman belief systems. The modern birthstone list most commonly referred to is from the American National Association of Jewellers, and was adopted in 1912. The following is a cumulative list of commonly-accepted zodiac birthstones.

Zodiac Birthstones

Zodiac Sign	Dates	Birthstone
Aries	Mar. 21 - Apr. 20	Bloodstone, Diamond
Taurus	Apr. 21 - May 21	Sapphire, Amber, Emerald, Azurite
Gemini	May 22 - Jun. 21	Agate, Chrysoprase, Citrine, Moonstone, Pearl
Cancer	Jun. 22 - Jul. 22	Emerald, Moonstone, Pearl, Ruby
Leo	Jul. 23 - Aug. 23	Onyx, Carnelian, Sardonyx, Tourmaline
Virgo	Aug. 24 - Sep.22	Carnelian, Jade, Jasper, Sapphire
Libra	Sep. 23 - Oct. 23	Peridot, Lapis Lazuli, Opal
Scorpio	Oct. 24 - Nov. 22	Beryl, Apache Tear, Aquamarine, Topaz
Sagittarius	Nov. 23 - Dec. 21	Topaz, Amethyst, Ruby, Sapphire, Turquoise
Capricorn	Dec. 22 - Jan. 20	Ruby, Agate, Garnet, Black Onyx
Aquarius	Jan. 21 - Feb. 18	Garnet, Amethyst, Moss Agate, Opal
Pisces	Feb. 19 - Mar. 20	Amethyst, Aquamarine, Rock Crystal

Metal Affinities

Planet-metal affinities have also been known for eons, and are used in alchemy, homeopathy, and astrology. Consider using metals in the same way you would use traditional birthstones. Metals hold an important place in manifesting – they receive, attract and communicate our desires. The follwing table may help you

Planet – Metal – Manifesting Links

Age	Planet	Metal	Zodiac Sign	Manifesting Qualities
Ancient	Sun	Gold	Leo	Attractor
	Moon	Silver	Cancer	Receiver
	Mercury	Mercury	Gemini/Virgo	Accelerator
	Venus	Copper	Taurus/Libra	Communicator
	Mars	Iron	Aries	Strengthener
	Jupiter	Tin	Sagittarius	Motivator
	Saturn	Lead	Capricorn	Converter
Modern	Uranus	Zinc	Aquarius	Generator
	Neptune	Platinum	Pisces	Completer
	Pluto	Bismuth	Scorpio	Transmitter

focus more positive energy into your manifesting techniques. Perhaps this is the first time you have thought about a metal in this way. If so, consider which metals you have in your home. Personal preference is so often based on aesthetic value, and while those responses within us are important, consider also how you feel when wearing different metals or being in close proximity to them.

Remember to come back to this list when creating your own manifesting jewelery, which will be discussed in the chapter entitled 'Manifesting with Crystals: Techniques'.

Day of the week gems are also considered lucky in many parts of the world. Which day of the week were you born, fair of face or loving and giving? There is a stone allocated for each the day of the week, which may resonate with you:

Monday - Pearl	Tuesday - Garnet	Wednesday - Cat's Eye
Thursday - Emerald	Friday - Topaz	Saturday - Sapphire
	Sunday - Ruby	

Crystal Astrology

A modern way to discover a crystal that resonates specifically with you is through crystal astrology. With a minimum of fuss you can find out your birth day crystal. Visit www.crystalastrology.com to find out the crystal associated with your birth day. Simply enter your birth details and a Sabian Symbols and Crystals Natal Report pops up, with the first crystal in the list being your birth day crystal. This crystal is linked to the specific degree of the sun when you were born. This crystal correlates to your sun, and promotes personal power, good fortune, karmic direction, and native abilities. Crystal Astrology also relates crystals to the moon and other planets in your astrology. Explore this concept more thoroughly by reading my book, *The Complete Guide to Crystal Astrology*. I believe we are now firmly within the ascension process, and that we all have a greater capacity to understand, and a greater desire to know, than ever before.

Another way to find your personal sacred stone is to go to a crystal worker or a crystal shop and take some time to discover which crystals help you feel 'in sync'. The right crystal will energize you; you will feel connected to the crystal; it will call out to you. If you are focussed, you will have strong and certain feelings about which crystal is your personal sacred stone.

Where to Go to Find Your Crystals

Of course, all good crystal shops have a vast selection of crystals. The owners of good crystal shops (on line or physical shops) choose their stock with loving care; they send out a strong intention, a request to the Universe and the crystals, to find the best specimens for them and for their future clientele. Shop owners use both their practical knowledge of gemstones and crystals and their intuitive sense to select crystals. They take the time to pass their hand over all the crystals they have available to them and sense which ones should be purchased for their sale collection. It is usually quite simple – the crystals will vibrate, look very very shiny, have a distinct inner glow, and in many cases jump off or roll off the display case if they are passed over.

The biggest gem show in the world is the Tucson Gem and Mineral Show™. It offers an extraordinary mineral, gem, fossil, lapidary and jewellry experience by bringing together specimens from all around the world. This show also brings together many crystal workers and crystal enthusiasts, and is the perfect place to experience, learn and share crystal lore. If you can't make it to Tucson, keep an eye out for local gem and mineral shows as they often bring crystals from Tuscon to you. By visiting your local gem and mineral show, you get an opportunity to experience many different crystals, many you may not have been aware of. And I guarantee you will meet a kindred spirit who will share their crystal stories with you.

Online shopping is also a very convenient way to shop for crystals. Just make sure there is a true and accurate picture of the crystal on the website, with the size and price clearly marked and payment options to suit you. Look for a site that allows returns and refunds, just in case when you get your crystal it is not what you had hoped for. Contact the seller if you have any questions, and in particular ask where the crystal has come from and if it has been enhanced or treated in any way. The best online stores include a metaphysical explanation for the crystal energies, and a statement saying that every effort has been made to source ethically mined and traded specimens. My favorite stores are listed in the back of this book.

Stepping outside is an amazing way to find your new crystal friend. Your local area may have some wonderful hidden treats including Seashells, river Pebbles, and other Rocks and Stones. Walking along a river bank, on a ridge top, or along a roadside offers opportunities to find a stone just for you. It is not important that you know the stone's 'real' name; of course you could do some research to discover its name, but what is more important is how the stone resonates with you, what appeals to you about it, and how it makes you feel. If you start to make crystal collecting a hobby, be sure to check whether fossicking permits are required in the area you are searching and always obtain the necessary permission.

Two wonderful examples of real treasures you can find in your natural environment are heart stones and holey stones. Heart stones are stones that have been weathered by time and the elements into a heart shape. These natural gifts raise self appreciation and love; they empower your heart to be guided into a place of strength and confidence. Holey stones are stones that have a hole within the stone, that has been naturally worn away by time and the elements. Believed to contain ancient wisdom, holey stones are known for their ability to heal and protect.

Visit crystals in public galleries, private collections, museums of natural history, universities, and specialized geo-museums such as the Clausthaler GeoMuseum. Such collections offer an exceptional opportunity to get close to a diverse range of perfect, large, extremely rare, and aesthetically appealing minerals and gems.

Presents are always welcome, but when it is a beautiful crystal the gift is even more special. A crystal gift received from a loved one, from a friend, as a result of a trade, or as a lucky find, is the Universe's way of manifesting help for something you really need assistance with. Accepting gifts is sometimes hard; accepting a true gift from another person or the Universe allows the heart to expand, the spirit to brighten and energy to shift. Unsolicited gifts are always gratefully received.

You may feel drawn to tumbled stones, native crystals, cut stones, carved stones or naturally worn crystals. Use your intuition to assess which crystal forms you prefer, and through them endeavour to learn more about yourself. Using your own in-built guidance system and universal energy patterns, you will come to accept and appreciate your unique talents and gifts, all of which will enhance your ability to manifest positivity.

Now you know where to look for your crystal, keep in mind that you don't have to take all your crystal finds home with you. Pictures, memories and an energetic imprint are valuable in your manifesting quest; obtaining a trophy is not. Connect to a particular crystal in a meaningful way, acknowledge the crystal you have found, send it gratitude and love, and then leave it (in nature or in the museum) with the hope that another person will gain as much happiness from its discovery as you have, and knowing that you can re-connect to its energy when you need to.

Simple Recharging Techniques

The connection between you and your crystals may need re-charging at times. When you feel less connection to a crystal, when the crystal looks or feels dull, when your appreciation of the crystal diminishes, or life seems to be going awry, it may be time to re-charge your crystals.

Place crystal(s) in direct moonlight, near a candle, near a water feature, or move the crystal to a new location. Some crystals, like Quartz, can readily be washed in warm water, while other crystals will dissolve in water. Gemstone jewellry needs to be cleaned carefully, according to the needs of the stones within the jewellry, but does require regular cleaning. Smudging, music, coloured lamps, Reiki and prayer can also be used to recharge your crystals. *Purifying Crystals* by Michael Gienger[2] is a wonderful book that goes into detail on how to purify, recharge, energize and clean your crystals so that you can re-connect to your crystals and get the most out of your relationship with them.

The time it takes to re-establish a positive connection to your crystal could vary from a few hours to many years, and depends on the journey you have been on together and how deeply you have been connected to the crystal.

Some people are sensitive and attuned to crystal energies; but if you lack confidence, consult a crystal worker. With practice and exposure to crystals your skills will grow – your intuition and personal crystal interconnectivity will crystallize. Remember, you know the answers to your questions already; they are in your knowing and in your aura; you are in the process of uncovering a sacred personal truth, giving birth to future potential. You will find that as life experience influences the person you are, you may move through several personal crystals, but each one will remain special in your aura and memory.

Your new crystal companion may be a sapphire or a simple stone, but it *will* help you reach your goals.

Manifesting With Crystals: Techniques

Creating your own original, resourceful, intuitive and imaginative manifesting techniques is the most powerful way to create change in your life. But where should you start? In this chapter we look at various techniques for manifesting with crystals, including; crystal candles, candles in crystals, scent and crystals, water features, gem elixirs, meditation, massage, music and jewellery. Remember to utilize the crystal tools you have at home – crystals and accessories you already own have come to you at this time and place for this purpose. Oh, and of course have fun!

The Complete Guide to Manifesting with Crystals provides a framework for your new manifesting methods. Grab a pencil and jot down notes next to the tables in the next few pages to see what you own and how the crystals and jewellery you own are working in your life. The following tables summarize how metals, colours and crystal types can help you in your quest to manifest positive change in your life.

Metal Manifesting Qualities	
Metal	*Manifesting Qualities*
Gold	Gold **attracts** (positives and negatives)
Silver	Silver **receives** (positives and negatives)
Titanium	Titanium **accelerates** change
Copper	Copper enhances **communication** through thoughts and words
Iron	Iron **strengthens** personal resolve
Stainless steel	Stainless steel **motivates**
Platinum	Platinum **completes**

Be aware that metals react to both the positive and the negative. The key is for you to fill your life with positive feelings, thoughts, actions, will and energy so that the metal in your jewellery can bring you positive changes. If you choose to surround yourself with positivity, the metals listed above will help attract, accelerate and motivate positive change. If you have negative thoughts and make poor choices, the metals you wear will amplify, attract and motivate more negativity in your life. Which metals are you normally drawn to? And has this now changed since viewing the table?

Another valuable quality to assess is the dominant colours of crystals you own. For example, your jewellery may have a dominant colour theme, with seven out of ten pieces being either gold or blue. Or you may have many white crystals and very few brown crystals. In manifesting, you can work with the dominant colour scheme in the same way you can work with colour therapy in aura integration and chakra balancing. In the following table, you might like to place a tick next to the colours you have identified in your crystals.

Colour Manifesting Qualities		
Colour	Activates Chakra	Manifests
Red	Root	Energy and passion
Orange	Sacrum	Joy and creativity
Yellow	Solar Plexus	Personal power and intelligence
Green	Heart	Prosperity and harmony
Blue	Throat	Communication
Indigo	Third Eye	Intuition
Violet	Crown	Divine connectivity
White		Purity and wisdom
Black		Power and force
Coral/Peach		Love and harmony
Gold		Alchemy and magic
Silver		Reflection and grace
Pink		Gentleness and healing
Turquoise		Communication and comprehension
Brown/cream/olive		Environmental awareness and grounding

What colour jewellery and crystals dominate your life? How might you incorporate new colours into your life?

There are hundreds of different crystal types and the table below deals with just a very few. This table is a simple guide for the top eleven life situations in which people usually seek help for manifesting positive change.

Crystal Manifesting Qualities	
Crystal	Manifests positive change in
Amethyst or Quartz	Spirituality
Rhyolite or Fluorite	Family
Angelite or Peridot	Children
Kunzite or Chrysoprase	Relationships
Malachite or Amazonite	Learning
Fluorite or Moss Agate	Health
Agate or Opal	Creativity
Lapis Lazuli or Jade	Finances
Aventurine or Sapphire	Career
Emerald or Larimar	Fame

There is a crystal index at the back of the book that links over eighty crystals with associated life experiences, including manifesting new beginnings, success and clarity.

All crystal forms – natural crystals, tumbled stones, spheres, beads, geodes, slices and cut crystals – can be used in crystal manifesting techniques. However, there are four shapes that have a special place in manifesting: the Merkaba, the pyramid, the egg and the sphere.

The Merkaba is the shape of a star tetrahedron – two intertwined, three-sided pyramids that form a three-dimensional Star of David. A powerful manifesting tool, it unites the mind, heart and body to move light and energy into the soul. This symbol balances needs with desires. You can find a Merkaba shaped from metal or crystal. If you are fortunate and a Merkaba makes its way to you, treat it with honour and respect.

Pyramids are another shape the collective unconsciousness recognizes. The pyramid strengthens your mind and guides your spiritual evolution. The pyramid helps you focus clear energies from the Divine into your life, fostering expansion through change. When you find yourself alone, rundown and feeling purposeless, the pyramid will restructure and restore your energy.

Crystal eggs represent fertility, birth, and rebirth. The egg shape manifests transformation and is a productive/reproductive symbol. When you are planning a completely new project or looking for fertile outcomes, utilize your crystal eggs.

The sphere is another very potent shape. It heightens insight, intuition, healing and divination. The sphere helps you see into the past, define the present, and predict the future. It brings unrealized potentials into reality, and represents the space you need to accomplish your goals. Work responsibly with the sphere and your inner world will manifest.

The Merkaba, pyramid, egg and sphere have been known to appear in dreams, where the image is seen to emblazon the aura or a portion of the body. If you have this experience, it is an auspicious sign - move forward with confidence, manifesting positive change in your life.

Candles and Crystals

Candles and crystals* blend the elements of fire, air and earth into one powerful manifesting technique. Crystal candles are candles that have had a crystal placed within the candle during production, or have crystals placed on the top surface of the crystal while burning. In either case, *the crystal is within the candle*. Crystal candles activate thoughts, action and will. If you focus positive feelings and energy while the candle is burning, crystal manifesting will be at its most potent. This technique focuses on the fire element, energizing the Will.

Making your own crystal candle requires a bit of creativity. You may choose to make a candle and place a crystal inside it, or you can add small crystals (chips) to the top of the candle as it melts. You can also purchase crystal candles, my favourite being the Brilliant Spheres Crystals, Crystal Candles™ (www.brilliant spherescrystals.com.au). Unique and effective, these candles have a precious tumbled stone within them, and the lit candle radiates the energy of the crystal contained within. They come in many varieties including: Amethyst for inspiration, Aquamarine for hope, Citrine for abundance, Fluorite for understanding, Hematite for release, Lapis lazuli for expanding, Rose Quartz for love, Tourmaline for optimism, Jade for Balance and Carnelian for concentration.

Choose a crystal candle that suits your needs. Plan what positive affirmation you will say when lighting the candle, and hold positive thoughts while you let the candle burn. For example, let's choose the Crystal Candle™ Citrine for abundance.

* Please note: Always supervise burning candles, particularly when children and pets are around. Take care that candles have a stable base so they can't tip over and ignite surrounding flammable materials.

The Positive Feeling:
I FEEL GRATITUDE FOR THE BEAUTY OF THIS MOMENT.

The Positive Thought:
I INVITE PROSPERITY INTO MY FUTURE.

The Positive Action:
I MANAGE MY LIFE TO INCLUDE SPACE TO GENERATE WEALTH.

The Positive Will:
THIS CANDLELIGHT IS MOTIVATING CONFIDENCE IN MY BEING.

The Positive Energy:
I AM AT THE CROSSROADS OF TODAY AND MY BRILLIANT FUTURE; I CHOOSE
TO RE-CONNECT WITH ETERNAL POSSIBILITIES.

Crystal candles are best utilized to manifest a change in your Will. Fire promotes movement, confidence, generosity and enthusiasm. If you have your ideas and plans ready to manifest, crystal candles push that change to happen.

You may have seen a tea light that sits inside a crystal, often Rose Quartz or Clear Quartz. This is an example of *a candle within a crystal.* Sandstone candle holders and Himalayan salt lamps are also examples of candles in crystals. Candles in crystals are stunning to behold, and create a beautiful play of light inside the crystal that energizes the whole room. The emphasis with this technique is energizing the earth element, motivating Action.

It is quite simple to create your own candles in crystals. Select your candle, place it in the middle of a small plate, and then surround the tea light with your own crystals. This has a two-fold effect; you are re-energizing your crystals while manifesting.

Consider the following example: A tea light is surrounded by a variety of yellow and orange crystals, which may include Orange Aventurine, Yellow Quartz, Citrine, Gold jewellery, or yellow Glass. This example is to manifest abundance.

The Positive Feeling:
I FEEL LOVE FOR THE BEAUTY OF EVERYTHING.

The Positive Thought:
I CREATE PROSPERITY IN MY LIFE.

The Positive Action:
I GENERATE WEALTH THROUGH THE ACTIONS I DO.

The Positive Will:
I AM MOTIVATED AND ENERGIZED.

The Positive Energy:
MY NATURAL ABILITIES WILL SUPPORT MY ACCOMPLISHMENTS.

A candle in a crystal creates a shift, a change. The fire from the candle ignites your energy. Your energy then shifts you into a better space, and translates into manifesting positivity in your life.

Scent and Crystals

Scent – incense, aromatherapy, perfume – combined with crystal energy is another beautiful and powerful manifesting pairing. Incense, used for thousands of years to enhance spirituality, can also be used with crystals to enhance positive change. Aromatherapy, the knowledgeable use of pure essential and absolute oils for physical healing and emotional change, is also a natural partner for crystal energy. Perfumes, in all their forms, popular and natural, can be utilized too, but take careful note of the names and scents to be sure they resonate with your goals.

Crystals are best placed next to your perfume, aromatherapy burner, or incense holder. Also consider keeping a crystal next to essential oils in storage so as to raise the energy of the oil. Single essences like rose, lemon, orange and ylang ylang have specific attributes that you can use with single crystals to enhance the aromatherapy effects. You can also make or purchase essential oil blends and specific incense to manifest peace, love, harmony, cleansing and release. Aromatherapists, for example, create specific manifesting oil blends, and you can too. Make sure the oils you use are 100% pure essential oils and your incense is natural. A manifesting oil blend should resonate happily with your sense of smell and your intentions. Use crystal and scent to enhance an energy change in your home.

Examples:

To manifest abundance: A blend of lemon, bergamot and clary sage next to a crystal.

> **Crystal Hint for abundance:** Citrine

To manifest a romantic relationship: Rose geranium oil, ginger or jasmine next to a crystal.

> **Crystal Hint for romance:** Kunzite or Morganite

Water and Crystals

Water and crystals combine feelings (water) and action (crystals), facilitating the manifestation of your heart's desire through positive action. A natural water source is the most potent location for manifesting. Visiting such places as the ocean, a river, volcanic crater or a natural spring is nature's all-in-one answer. Natural locations provide energetically abundant rocks, crystals, sand and beauty, moving you to a space where you can create your new future. If the water and crystals manifesting technique resonates with you, consider creating your own water feature. Your water feature can be as simple as tumbled stones placed in a glass bowl with clean water, or as ornate as a large water feature in your garden. Sit by your water feature with your physical body relaxed, and your mind focused on your vision of the future.

Gem elixirs are also a magical way of bringing water and crystal energy together. Goebel and Gienger have written a beautiful book, *Gem Water: How to Prepare and Use Over 130 Crystal Waters for Therapeutic Treatments.*[3] Use the principals in this book if you want to combine water and crystals for healing, balancing and energizing. Take care when choosing which crystals you will place in or near water features or in gem elixirs. Quartz based crystals, including Amethyst, Citrine and Agate, are best suited to water features. Be aware that some crystals actually dissolve in water, and you don't want to lose a precious crystal!

Also, some crystals are toxic; if in doubt, please ask at your local crystal shop or do some research.

> **Crystal Hint for water feature:** Pebbles help you make the most of every opportunity

Carefully place pebbles in the base of a clear glass vase, and add a floating candle or a flower. With this combination, you are uniting earth, air, fire and water to create an emotional lift for yourself and your home.

Meditation and Crystals

Meditation can be a valuable part of your daily life. Meditation manifests positive changes. Meditation can be as short as a few seconds or as long as a retreat. Through mindfulness and concentration, you give yourself the freedom and time to explore new realities. A rest from your current reality may be just what you need to shift focus and open up new possibilities. Spiritual thinking through meditation leads to growth and personal ascension. Incorporate crystals into any meditation. You may choose to place crystals on your chakra centres or around your body, in a formation or randomly as your intuition guides you.

For those new to meditating: find a quiet and safe place, sit in a comfortable position, and hold a crystal that you have specifically chosen for this time and place. Breathe gently and relax. Focus on your crystal, noticing every detail, becoming the crystal in your imagination, filling your mind with its colour. Continue exploring the crystal until your eyes rest on a comfortable area. Experience the energy flow between you and the crystal. When you are ready to 'return', slowly become aware of things around you, place your crystal by your side and move your fingers and toes. Say a short prayer of gratitude to conclude your meditation.

> **Crystal Hint for meditation:** Alabaster (Onyx) promotes understanding, calmness and enlightenment

Massage and Crystals

Massaging with crystals can be done with the crystal touching the skin (crystal massage) or with the crystal placed next to or under the body (crystal healing). Crystals that lend themselves best to crystal massage are smooth crystals that slide over the skin; for example, spheres, eggs, tumbled rounds, and wands. Massage and crystals techniques really focus on mental and physical health and well-being, which in turn sets the stage for you and your ability to manifest positivity in your life. Michael Gienger has written a beautiful book, *Crystal Massage for Health and Healing,* [4] which delves into these techniques more thoroughly. Remember that when you are 'in sync' you are living in harmony with your heart's desire, and your ability to manifest positive outcomes is heightened.

Music and Crystals

Combine music with crystals by holding crystals in your hand while listening to relaxing or motivating music. In particular, listen to crystal singing bowls, bells and/or chimes, as these instruments are made to emit 'pure tones'. The music is healing vibrations resonating with your physical and spiritual body. The sound refines your energy, moving you into a higher awareness. When you are in tune, manifesting is easier.

Jewellery

Creating jewellery can be a unique and energizing way to manifest with crystals. For thousands of years people have adorned themselves with beautiful crystals, and fortunately this continues today. There are significant times in life when a gift of a special piece of jewellery makes an enormous difference. For instance, during childbirth a birthing bracelet or necklace might be given (Garnet); or in times of stress (Jasper) or grief (Moonstone) the right piece of jewellery can change a person's stamina, endurance and outlook. Crystallize your life, and help others crystallize their lives too. Might I suggest you really search your home for jewellery you already own, gather it together, and make a conscious effort to assess what resources you already have. Compare it with the tables earlier in this chapter and you may see patterns emerging that indicate why you are in the situation you are in, and how best to move forward.

Every moment, every thing around you interacts, repels and absorbs. Don't waste a moment. Try to include in your life some of the techniques already discussed. Make notes; create a crystal 'recipe' book of techniques you like and that work for you. When gratitude, love and confidence find their way into your life, good things happen.

Everyday Crystal Recipes

Here are a few easy crystal recipes to bring manifesting with crystal techniques into your daily life. With each one, begin by carefully selecting the crystals you wish to help you manifest positive outcomes.

✧ Place manifesting crystals next to your home computer monitor, with your screen saver set to scroll text across the screen. The text should indicate what you are trying to manifest; for example, *I feel satisfied that I am achieving my desires.*

✧ Place manifesting crystals near your shower recess, hand basin and bath. Scented soaps and music create an area where you can connect to your wishes. Seashells are particularly powerful in this environment as they invigorate your aura. (Remember to use crystals that will not dissolve; use Agate, for example.)

✧ Light incense or aromatherapy burners infused with crystal energy in living areas, the kitchen or bedroom to manifest your goals, and particularly next to your manifesting picture board.

✧ Place a crystal in the top drawer of your desk at work to help manifest positivity in your career. Write a positive mantra in your diary to keep your goals in mind. Make positive decisions to change your daily activities so as to enhance positive change.

✧ Leave a protection stone like Tiger Eye or Falcon Eye in the car; it will help you recognize important information and prompt you to act when you see warning signs in your life.

✧ Place a crystal in your work bag or your child's school bag. Malachite, Fluorite or Mookaite will assist learning, comprehension and optimism.

✧ Glue crystals onto a photo frame. Place in it a photo of yourself, a loved one or something dear to you, and hang the crystal frame in a prominent position. Lighting a candle near this photo enhances your positive thoughts.

✧ Add crystals (preferably quartz crystals) to garden pots near your front door to attract and grow positive energy.

When learning to manifest with crystals, be sure to focus on your individual goals and bettering your own situation before working with your partner, children or friends. When you are happy with the way your life is changing, you can start sharing your manifesting techniques with those you trust. You will find some of the techniques in this chapter resonate with you, others less so. Only you can assess which techniques *you* can manage effectively. Make a note of when you see your life changing for the better. With each crystal technique, remember the High Five:

Feelings	Water	Emotional Connectivity
Thoughts	Air	Positive Communication (with Clarity)
Actions	Earth	Positive Action (with Planning and Diligence)
Will	Fire	Movement (with Confidence and Enthusiasm)
Energy	Spirit	Fortitude and Determination

There is an extensive manifesting with crystals index at the back of the book that covers over eighty real-life experiences, including manifesting abundance, charm and fun, and lists the crystals that best assist positive change in the chosen area. Remember to be original and creative. Use the tools you have to hand before going out and buying things you may not need. Play around with various techniques and write down your crystal recipes for future use.

Manifesting world peace starts with the mind of one
and ends in the hearts of all.

Crystal Recipes
for Manifesting

Crystal recipes for manifesting should be fun and creative. They should utilize the things already in your life, and introduce some new experiences too. Here are some real-life examples of how to create some crystal manifesting recipes. Five crystal recipes are provided, to manifest Love, Prosperity, a Vocation, Health and Well-being, and Spirituality.

Each recipe includes:
✧ a list of ingredients that corresponds to the High Five
✧ an example of crystals to use in your recipe
✧ an example of written text to help you manifest change
✧ a mantra to help foster positive thought
✧ an activity to help invite positive change into your life

Feel free to replace any crystal with one you already own, and relocate the setting to a place easily accessible to you. I also suggest you refer to a Lo Shu Square as used in Feng Shui. The practice of Feng Shui balances the chi in your home, inviting positive energy into your future. Feng Shui outlines a path to manifesting through de-cluttering, which allows space for new things to enter your life.

The table below is a Lo Shu Square, a Feng Shui map for your house. The Lo Shu Square is used to analyse sectors in your home, and shows you how to divide your floor plan into nine equal-sized squares. The table below shows the Feng Shui sectors, and the colour and crystals that correspond to each sector. Align the bottom edge of the Lo Shu Square with your front door to locate the various sectors in your own home. If you have two or three floors in your home, use this Lo Shu Square for each level, with the bottom edge lined up with the ground floor. Most front doors are in the career/life path sector.

Wealth Sector	Fame Sector	Relationship Sector
turquoise - light blue	*red or purple*	*yellow - pink - orange*
Turquoise, Fluorite, Chrysoprase	Garnet, Amethyst, Ruby	Rose Quartz, Rhodocrosite, Kunzite
Family Sector	Health Sector	Creativity/Children Sector
green	*yellow - pink - peach*	*gold or silver*
Emerald, Dioptase, Jade	Carnelian, Amber, Yellow Calcite	Diamond, White Agate, White Onyx
Study/Meditation Sector	Career/Life Path Sector	Helpful Friends, Angels, Travel Sector
yellow - orange	*blue or black*	*white, magenta, metallic*
Rutilated Quartz, Mookaite	Aquamarine, Blue Lace Agate, Lapis Lazuli	Clear Quartz, Selenite, White Marble

Area *Colour* Crystal

As an example of how to use this table, place White Agate into your 'Children Sector' to enhance fertility. Place Carnelian in your 'Health Sector' to improve your health. The crystals suggested for each sector of your home resonate both with Feng Shui energy flow and colour therapy, harmoniously manifesting positivity in your life.

A Crystal Recipe to Manifest Love

Try this crystal recipe if manifesting positive outcomes in Love is one of your priorities at this time.

High Five	Feelings	Thoughts	Actions	Will	Energy
Elements	Water	Air	Earth	Fire	Spirit
Recipe	Love	Mantra	Feng Shui	Passion	Perfume

Crystals

Select and hold a crystal that best suits your relationship goal. Follow your intuition or use the suggestions below:

Friendship - Kunzite or Moonstone
Romance - Ruby or Morganite
Marriage - Diamond, Sapphire, Precious Metal
Soul Mate - Clear Crystals (Quartz, Diamond, Glass, etc.)

Setting

The best setting for this recipe is near water, be it the ocean, a river, or a small water feature in your home. Wear some crystal-enhanced perfume.

Letter

Use a black or red pen on pink tissue paper to write as much as you can about your wants and needs, as if your desires have already manifested in your life. Detail what it is you expect in a relationship, what you have to offer, and how grateful you are.

Hint: I have a fantastic person sharing my life; this person respects and loves me and our life is happy. Our relationship conveys honesty, loyalty and security. Our love deepens daily. We support each other in our life goals and karmic quest. I am generous, compassionate, understanding, and my love and confidence in our relationship grows and grows. I am so very grateful for the support, kindness and hope this person gives me and I show this in the little things I do for this person daily. From today forward I am changing my lifestyle so that new people enter and I see my old friends in a new light.

Mantra

Summarize your desire into one simple manifesting mantra, and vocalize it.
Hint: I am in love

Activity

Say your new mantra over and over, aloud at first, then, once you feel confident that the words are true, say the mantra in your mind. You may have a rush of emotion; feelings of sadness, loneliness and hopelessness may wash over you at first; then you will believe your words, and then love can manifest.

Place your letter in a visible location in the Feng Shui relationship sector of your home. Keep the crystal close to you at all times. Show yourself love and kindness when you notice the crystal and letter. Keep adding symbols of love to the Feng Shui relationship sector of your home.

A Crystal Recipe to Manifest Prosperity

Try this crystal recipe if manifesting positive outcomes in Prosperity is one of your priorities at this time.

High Five	Feelings	Thoughts	Actions	Will	Energy
Elements	Water	Air	Earth	Fire	Spirit
Recipe	Prosperity	Letter	Moneybox	Acquisition	Expansive

Crystals

Select and hold a crystal that best suits you for manifesting prosperity. Follow your intuition or use the suggestions below:

Finances – Lapis Lazuli, Citrine, Rutilated Quartz, Serpentinite, or a Precious Metal

Setting

The best setting for this recipe is a public park, preferably where large boulders are visible. You can re-create this setting in your home by gathering your larger crystals and placing them together on green fabric. Make sure your wallet has only money and important personal information in it. (Remove bills, receipts and junk from your wallet.)

Letter

Use a black or gold pen on green or yellow coloured paper to write as much as you can about your wants and needs, as if your desires have already manifested in your life. Detail what it is you are looking for in your life, what you have to offer, and how grateful you are.

Hint: I am constantly re-crystallizing myself through profitable interactions. I feel prosperous, safe and secure. Fortunate opportunities and good ethics lead me toward successful promotions. I have enough money to sustain my soulful life, with plenty to share. I make positive decisions that echo into other people's lives and manifest happiness around me. I am generous and will continue to share my generosity as my income increases, as I know blessings and kindness make for a happier path to follow. I am very grateful for having been born into my life and for living in this country. I am grateful for the opportunities in my life.

Mantra

Summarize your desire into one simple manifesting mantra, and vocalize it.
Hint: I am prosperous.

Activity

Say your new mantra over and over, aloud in the beginning, and then in your mind, as you feel confident the words are true. Believe in your words.

Write your mantra on yellow paper and keep it in your wallet. Place your letter in a box that you decorate with crystal chips and pictures of things you spend your money on. Place your moneybox where you would normally put your bills, usually on an accessible tabletop. Relocate your bills to a filing system in the home office. Keep a small crystal in your bill file. Place small change, coupons and investment information into your moneybox.

A Crystal Recipe to Manifest a Vocation

Try this crystal recipe if manifesting positive outcomes in your Vocation is one of your priorities at this time.

High Five	Feelings	Thoughts	Actions	Will	Energy
Elements	Water	Air	Earth	Fire	Spirit
Recipe	Individuality	Letter	Skills	Candle	Music

Crystals

Select and hold a crystal that best suits you for an improvement in your career. Follow your intuition or use the suggestions below:

Vocation - Aventurine, Sapphire, Shells, Glass, or a Precious Metal

Setting

The best setting for this recipe is comfortable surroundings, and a white candle on which you have written in black ink the word 'Vocation'. Light the candle. Have your favourite music playing.

Letter

Use a black or blue pen on white office paper to write as much as you can about your wants and needs, as if your desires have already manifested in your life. Detail what it is you are looking for in your career, what you have to offer, and how grateful you are.

Hint: I am honest, polite and professional. I enjoy the career I have. My vocation is important to my self-esteem because it is an expression of who I am in my world. People know me by what I do. I enjoy being in a productive environment, my contributions make a difference, and I see things grow because of the job I do. Practical relationships manufacture opportunities to fulfil spiritual obligations. My specific skill set forms the basis for financial and spiritual reward. The work I do is offered as a prayer to a higher good; it is a gift of generosity for the life I live. People in my work environment are respectful, loyal and communicative. I am grateful to know my place in my world.

Mantra

Summarize your desire into a simple manifesting thought, and vocalize it.
Hint: I work with my natural abilities.

Activity

Say your new mantra over and over, aloud in the beginning, and then in your mind, as you feel confident the words are true. You may have a rush of emotion; acknowledge these emotions and guide them toward confidence and hope.

Place your letter with a crystal in the top drawer of your desk at work, particularly if you are looking for a promotion or a career change. Place it in the top drawer of your desk in your home office if are manifesting a new job and work/life balance. Update your CV and keep an eye on your marketability.

A Crystal Recipe to Manifest Health and Well-being

Try this crystal recipe if manifesting positive Health and Well-being are your priorities at this time.

High Five	Feelings	Thoughts	Actions	Will	Energy
Elements	Water	Air	Earth	Fire	Spirit
Recipe	Optimism	Photo	Plants	Candles	Breathing

Crystals

Select and hold a crystal that best suits you for an improvement in your health and well-being. Follow your intuition or use the suggestions below:

Health – Copper, Water Agate, Moss Agate, Green Fluorite
Happiness – Strawberry Quartz, Siberian Quartz, Aqua Aura, Gold Stone
Hope – Shiva-Lingham, Rainbow Fluorite

Setting

The best setting for this recipe is a small, secluded garden surrounded by natural light and healthy plants. If possible, safely place on the ground a photo of you when you were happy and healthy, and surround the photo with four lit tea lights. Breathe deeply and regularly, accepting the gift of energy from your beautiful surroundings.

Letter

Use a green or red pen on white office paper to write as much as you can about your wants and needs, as if your desires have already manifested in your life. Detail what it is you are looking for in the area of health, what you have now, and how grateful you are.

Hint: My optimism throughout life helps me and my loved ones grow in faith and love. My mature intentions nurture positive choices and good health. Open-mindedness, mental clarity and balance are liberating. I enjoy outdoor adventures. By uniting my mind, body and spirit, I restore my health and well-being. I am the harmony, balance and inner peace in my life. My interesting lifestyle stems from beneficial physical activity, meditation and visualization. I understand my own health. I accept help today. I assess all options to increase my healthy lifestyle.

Mantra

Summarize your desires into one simple manifesting thought, and vocalize it.
Hint: I live an enriching, nourishing, healthy life.

Activity

Create a picture board with pictures of you when you were feeling well and happy. Add pictures of holiday destinations, healthy food choices, recipes, beautiful scenes and planned outdoor activities. Create a collection of motivational music that you can play while exercising, making sure the music has meaning that is in tune with your health goals.

A Crystal Recipe to Manifest Spirituality

Try this crystal recipe to manifest positive Spiritual Development in your life.

High Five	Feelings	Thoughts	Actions	Will	Energy
Elements	Water	Air	Earth	Fire	Spirit
Recipe	Centred	Mantra	Chakras	Mandala	Ascended Masters

Crystals

Select and hold a crystal that best suits you for an improvement in your spiritual development. Follow your intuition or use the suggestions below:

Spirituality – Amethyst, Spinel, Rose Quartz, Amegreen, Sodalite

Setting
Sit comfortably at a table indoors and make a mandala. You can create an image or download one from the Internet. Light your favourite candle and place it on the table where you are working.

Mandala
Fill in all the areas of the mandala – colour in, use glue and coloured sand, and/or use glue to attach crystal chips. The construction of your own personal mandala creates a sense of unity and wholeness, awakening and developing your spirit. Collect from your crystal collection coloured stones to resonate with your chakra centres (red, orange, yellow, green/pink, blue, purple, white).

Mantra
Hint: I am present in this moment. My mind is filled with wonder and awe for all that is seen and unseen. I am grateful for this moment.

Activity
Take your mandala and chakra crystals and find a place to lie down comfortably and safely, either inside or outside. Place the mandala at your feet, lie down, and place the chakra stones on your chakra centres. Create a prayer to say while lying down. Visualize the representatives of the spiritual belief system you hold, be that Angels, Jesus, Buddha, Kwan Yin and/or other Ascended Masters. Spend some time in quiet meditation, gently drawing your attention to your chakra centres as time passes. Place images of Ascended Masters inside your home to remind you that you are never alone.

Banking Positivity

Life is great when things go our way, when what we plan for comes to fruition and the road we travel is well lit. But we all know life can have its share of challenges, when an unexpected turn of events changes the life we know, potentially forever. Our desire to be incarnated on this planet at this time must be so that we can live, experience, learn and grow, or else why would we be here? But, to be sure, our view of life can change depending on what kind of day we are having and what challenges come our way. The view from the mountaintop of ecstasy is very different from the dark cave of grief and despair, and it is in that darkness that a safety rope, a karmic nest egg or a bank of positivity comes in handy.

Banking positivity is a concept similar to putting money away for a rainy day. It requires that you invest in yourself, which in turn requires a few simple things including respect and love for the individual you are and the life you live. Banking positivity is to know what makes you happy, and then practice being happy. It's similar to exercising your body; when you have a healthy body you recover quickly from illness. When you bank positivity you recover quickly from the curve balls life throws. Remember, the curve balls give us opportunities to be teachers to our children, our family and workmates, and show people what an advanced soul looks like. Incorporate positive changes in your day, bank positivity, and you will begin to see the glass half full, especially on 'those days'.

Do you know yourself well enough to know what makes you happy? If this is your first step towards knowing who you have become in your busy world, and what now makes you happy, try meditating with Serpentinite cupped in your hands. Serpentinite reveals your essential self by re-crystallizing, synthesizing and integrating your past, present and future so that you can transform into an ultimate state of being.

Imagine two different lifestyles for yourself. In the first lifestyle you spend a portion of every day crying and being upset. What is being banked in that life? Despair and hopelessness. Those we love most may support this practice, giving us space to cry, holding us, comforting us; but by doing so they allow the repetition to go on, sometimes for many years. Those we love support this negative pattern because they love us and they don't know how else to help. Negative patterns driven by insecurity, trauma or fear decrease love, respect and honesty in a relationship, and often we take the ones who care for us for granted. A great deal of wasted energy and time, as well as falsehood, occurs in this person's life, and manifesting will not come easily.

In the second lifestyle you spend a portion of every day smiling, looking at clouds, gardening, talking to friends. In this life you are banking positivity for yourself and your family; you are making positive changes in your life, making positive routines and setting yourself up for a successful future. Small positive changes to daily activities will move you into a place where manifesting is much simpler. Being positive softens the experiences in life you were not ready for. Banking positivity is a valuable investment in your long-term well-being. Make a plan to rescue yourself from your own fears and anxieties. In dark days you can draw on your 'bank' by remembering how it feels to be positive. You will be an expert.

Practical Ways to Bank Positivity

Manifesting a real and positive shift in your life requires that you change how you currently live your life. The Universe is knocking, asking you to open new doors and try new things, to remove old worn-out things and in turn create a space for good things to enter your life. This may be as simple as a thorough clearout of your home, recycling clothes and furniture, or it may be a clearout of poor habits, depressing dialogue, difficult people, or the clearing of past life karma. A crystal in your pocket will ease your path when you are trying something new.

> **Crystal Hint for trying something new:** Lepidolite, Picasso Jasper, Opal.

Let go...

Manifest more by managing what you have wisely. Try not to hang onto things for 'best' – use them now. If you are in a 'waiting' state of mind, manifesting will wait too. Around you change is constant, healthy and normal. If you find you are hanging onto too many old, obsolete things or routines, you are manifesting a static pattern. Assess what is around you, and with careful consideration, see how the things around you make you feel. If there are negative feelings associated with various items, people or rituals, modify them slowly with kindness and gentleness. Cleansing is one of the most powerful manifesting techniques, and when you make it a practice it becomes one of many ways to bank positivity. Placing a crystal next to certain items helps clear the energy you and that item share.

> **Crystal Hint for letting go**: Blue Calcite, Yellow Calcite and Watermelon Tourmaline.

Keep a diary...

Keep a diary of your life; it will serve as a barometer for how well you are feeling and how you are travelling through life. Clearly communicate your goals in your diary, what progress you are making toward your goals, and any feelings of reward when you employ practical gratitude. Remember to reward yourself for accepting and releasing painful events. Attach a crystal to the front of your diary to enhance honest communication.

> **Crystal Hint for honest communication**: Ammolite, Turquoise.

Keep a dream journal...

An extension of the diary theme is the creation of a dream journal, where you record and analyse your dreams. A dream journal focuses on the dreams you have at night and the details they contain. Keep your dream journal near your bed with crystals glued to the cover to promote restful sleep and sweet dreams.

> **Crystal Hint for restful sleep and sweet dreams**: Ruby, Fuchsite, Celestite, Selenite.

Both your diary and dream journal act as road signs in your life, and enhance your understanding of consequences. With crystal energy working with you and your writing, ideas will manifest into reality.

Create a treasure box ...

Banking positivity, particularly for situations surrounding loss, can be an important part of living. A memory treasure box is a powerful way to focus your emotions; fill it with special photos, small trinkets, your favourite essential oils, some money, Citrine and Clear Quartz, an inspirational book, and other things you know you don't need on a daily basis but want to keep. Put your treasure box in a place you don't normally access, like the back of the linen cupboard. Keep the box there as a safety net. Bring your box out on anniversaries, Christmas or birthdays to celebrate the beauty you remember and the possibilities for your future. Each anniversary, write yourself a letter. Write down the best and worst of what you are feeling and keep it in the box. This exercise has long-term benefits, and you may be surprised how helpful it can be.

Share your life with a pet ...

Owning and caring for a pet is probably the most common way to bank positivity. The love your pet offers is unconditional, and yet they need you, and of course you need them. Pets radiate beauty, charm and love. Pets dissolve socio-economic boundaries; walking with a dog, for example, brings you into contact with all kinds of people on the street. Relating to our pets on an emotional and physical level reduces stress and promotes a happier lifestyle. If you communicate verbally with your pet you are more likely to experience a happier life. If you don't or can't own a pet, regularly pet sit for some one who does. You and your pet deserve support with crystals – while holding a crystal in your hand, stroke and/or look lovingly at your pet.

> **Crystal Hint to support you and your pets:** Rose Quartz, Smokey Quartz, Sugilite or Turquoise.

Take care of yourself ...

So many men and women get a new 'hair do' when they are faced with life-changing experiences. A relationship ends, maybe you choose a new colour; before starting a new job or on that big birthday, maybe you choose a new style. This is another form of banking positivity; it is a routine that provides a positive experience. Re-visiting your appearance, particularly your hair, is a physical manifestation of your aura, of your spirit transforming. A new style is a way for you to show others how you are feeling, changing and growing. A good hairdresser realizes this. They help you re-define who you are, help you make a change, and thereby allow positivity to manifest in your life. Hairdressers can point you in the right direction regarding a cut, a colour and a style, which directly translates to a boost in confidence.

Before going to have your hair cut, spend a few moments considering what it is you are looking for in your life and how your 'new do' can help you. It is quite common for people to react emotionally if they are not comfortable with their new look; its more than just a hair cut or colour, it is a shift in your energy brought about by someone else – quite powerful really. Be kind to yourself when you see your reflection after your hair cut, look beyond the physical and be open to new possibilities. Crystals in your bag when visiting the hairdressers will support a positive transformation.

> **Crystal Hint for positive transformation:** Pyrolusite, Pink Lace Agate, Rhodonite, Tiger Eye.

Dear Hairdresser,
Thank you for helping all the people you help. You are amazing. You listen and care; you revamp people on the inside and out. You are counsellor, stylist, confidante, best friend; your clients trust you. Please keep your spirit healthy so you can re-create, shape and beautify your clients' spirit. Consider keeping crystals in your salon, in a water feature, pot plant, or hidden from view if necessary. You need to look after your well-being and your business to continue providing your valuable service.
Crystal Blessings,
Your Clients

> **Crystal Hint for the well-being of a business:** Amethyst, Rose Quartz, pebbles, stainless steel or mirrors.

Using crystals in your daily life, while cooking, gardening, listening to music, cleaning and shopping, can support you in your quest to manifest positivity in your life. Banking positivity is a way to experience life without getting stuck in that dark corner. Make sure you have something prepared, something familiar, something you enjoy that can help you out of a dark place. Set your intention, create a plan, spend time and effort on your well-being. Promise yourself that you will look after your future. Your potential is the culmination of the best of your past plus the best of the opportunities in your future. Keep an eye on your life with the perspective of an eagle; keep an eye on the big picture.

Happiness is something you can manifest and manage. A few special people in your life can help you with finding happiness, people who support you in your goals, managers at work who value your contribution and professionalism, a loving partner and a happy family; they all lend themselves to a happy life. However, there is a little spark that needs to be kept alight in your own heart in order to be happy, for which only you can be responsible. Crystals can help that spark ignite and burn in a beneficial way.

> **Crystal Hint for happiness:** Chalcopyrite and Siberian or Aqua Aura quartz types.

Milestones in Life

They don't call them milestones for nothing. Milestones are markers along the road of life that help us and those we know assess how far we have come and how far we have to go. Everyone will have milestones that are important to them, be it their first kiss, the birth of a child, winning a sporting event, their 5th Christmas; however, most of us share a certain number of milestones similar to the ones listed below. A 'mile' is paired up with a 'stone' here to help you manifest positivity, peace and balance during this aspect of personal development.

Childbirth. The crystal for the mother is **Garnet** for vitality and confidence. The metal for the father is **Silver** to establish continuity. The crystal for the baby is **Clear Quartz** to support positive opportunities. This is a celebration of new life and new beginnings.

1ˢᵗ birthday or 1ˢᵗ anniversary. Crystals include **Ammolite** to enhance the natural rhythms and cycles of life, or **clear crystals** to support positivity. This is a celebration of the completion of a first cycle.

7ᵗʰ birthday. The crystal is **Angelite**, which guides and guards the child. The 7ᵗʰ birthday is when a child's spirit starts to form independently.

21ˢᵗ birthday. The crystal is the **personal birthstone**, which supports one's personal life path. This is when society's expectations and one's personal ego start to interact.

28ᵗʰ birthday. The crystal is **Tiger Eye** for protection and boundary setting. This is the spiritual beginning of the adult years and also the saturn return.

The big 0's (30, 40, 50, 60, 70, etc.). These big milestones are the times for a treat. **Pink Lace Agate** and/or **Howlite** will enhance gratitude and acceptance.

Marriage. Crystals include; **Morganite, Diamond, Sapphire** and **Ruby**. These crystals strenghten love, honesty and loyality.

Death of a loved one. Such a moment requires that one change enormously and quickly. Crystals that will support the transition for those that have suffered the loss of a loved one include **Iolite, Black Marble, Jet** and **Lead Crystal**.

Divorce. Crystals include **Halite, Jet** and **coloured Glass**. These crystals evaporate blocks, expose truths and purify the future.

Release (addictions, habits, relationships). Invite **Aventurine** or **Chrysocolla** into your life to help support confidence and negate self judgement.

Education. All phases of education will benefit from **Amazonite** as it aids verbal and written skills.

First day of school. Mangano Calcite promotes an atmosphere of cooperation and respect.

Transition to high school. Both Agate and Jasper promote skill, balance, determination and success.

Transition to college and university. Both Malachite and Azurite enhance concentration, visualisation, and wisdom.

Transition into the work force. Aventurine promotes self confidence and good fortune.

Transition out of the work force. Obsidian fosters new opportunities.

Financial transactions. Citrine enhances positive financial dealings.

Travelling. Tektite brings positive experiences when travelling.

Spirituality. White Gold provides a continual flow of light.

The crystals above are suggestions, and you may already have favourite crystals that you have received at specific milestones that differ from this list. Your family milestones create your group memories and support your spirit in low energy times. Share your favourite milestones and associated rituals with loved ones. It is important for you to recognize the crystals that have come into your life and acknowledge their role in your growth. Crystals are fantastic companions on your life path; trust that they support you in your goal to be successful.

Celebrating milestones invites graceful change into your life. Remain light-hearted and confident in life's ups and downs. Your higher awareness, attuned by crystal clarity, will help you in all situations. Acknowledge the support crystals offer to you. Choose to illuminate and modify you current circumstances to invite positive changes into your life. You can manifest positivity. You deserve for good things to happen to you.

Divine Perspective

What is your belief system? How did it develop? It is a beautiful experience to come to realize what Divinity means to you. Every event in your life has led you to the belief systems you have. Usually the more challenging your life, the more opportunity you will have to realize your own Divinity. Whether you believe in an external Divinity, an internal Divinity, or a combination of both, take some time to reconnect to the Divine and see your life from that perspective.

Divine perspective means accepting that the tapestry of your life looks perfect, even when all you can see is the unfinished underside where all the loose threads and gaps are visible. Divine perspective offers you a chance to step back and access your life with unconditional love, or at least the closest we humans can get to it. A degree of impartiality allows a clear look at the things that trigger anxiety, anger and stress in your life. Divine perspective is the space that you can place between you and a negative reaction to a situation. Try and respond to negative triggers as if you were sitting on another planet; in the grand scheme of things most challenges will only upset you if you allow them to. Divine perspective also helps you see with crystal clarity which key things are best manifested at which time.

With divine perspective both the diamond and the river pebble have magical potential and a divine purpose, as do you, your family, your friends and your neighbours. Everyone who shares your life at this time has meaning and purpose. Every soul is valuable. Every event and every moment has ramifications that potentially increase your enjoyment of life. Remember you are as beautiful as the energy that is in each and every crystal.

> **Crystal Hint for Divine perspective:** Banded Iron Stone, Meteorite, Damburite

Even though you may know you are ready to manifest positive change in your life, moving forward with your plan may feel like a step into the unknown. Be a willing participant in your new life and remember to keep focused. Stay true to the choices you make, and be gentle with the new you as you grow. Let go of old, negative, internal dialogue and patterns. Continue your new, positive, internal and external dialogue and manifest your reality. Above all, be kind to yourself and love your life. Your life can change. Your life *is* changing. Strange, new and wonderful experiences are on the horizon.

Even small, positive changes to your daily activities will make manifesting much easier. Staying in your routines leaves little space for new things to come in. Alternative routes can open up through new encounters; fresh ideas; different paths in thought, vision and action. So take the stairs rather than the lift, visit a park, try a new café, visit new shops - one little change can open the door upon which you have been knocking.

You have the tools, ability and desire to manifest. It is time to visualize and conceive your new future. Practice positive affirmations, positive speech, manifesting mantras and creative picture boards, and make use of the extra energy and motivation that crystal energy can add to your day. Regularly revisit techniques that combine crystals with mantras, candles, water, music, aromatherapy, massage and meditation. By taking the time and making an effort to change your routines, you are showing the Universe that you are ready for new things to emerge. Keep the techniques simple and fun - this is your life; you deserve the best.

So many priorities: buy a new computer, live a healthy lifestyle, earn more money, travel, fall in love, strengthen personal relationships, release hurt, pray more, learn to dance, purchase a home, gain confidence, speak in public, find a new job, renovate... Each positive outcome will require your energy and positivity. Remain balanced and aware. Use meditation time to refocus your energy. Look to your crystals for inspiration, and see them as friends who support you in living the life you want and deserve.

Changing your current patterns may require you to slow down and become mindful. Start a new pattern by introducing new plans, and allow evolution to happen. Repeating this positive affirmation will help if you feel unsettled:

I am strong.
I am in control of the choices I make.
I know which way to go.

Crystal Hint to provide hope during change: Shiva-Lingham, Rainbow Fluorite

---

Positive action, focused intention, crystal energy and timing attract positive outcomes in your life. Crystals work uniquely with you to support you higher purpose, by realigning intentions and focusing desires. Crystal Synchronization aligns time, energy and wishes to manifest positive changes, and promotes the awareness needed to ask for the right thing at the right time. As you become 'in sync', the things and events on your Karmic horizon will make their way to you, at just the right time. The more you experience this Divine timing, the more your confidence will grow. Manifesting a charmed life relies on your confidence, as well as your appreciation. Make time for playful and happy times. Make sure your life journey is filled with happiness by making positive choices.

Gratitude is the key to manifesting the things you desire. Spend some time every day looking at the beauty and love around you; this is vital for sustained happiness. When your mind wanders, try and refocus in a place where you feel happiness and gratitude. When you manifest something, give thanks in practical ways; by doing so, you will strengthen your connectivity with the world, open up to new opportunities and increase the flow of universal energy into your life.

Symbols and signs in your life show you where your life path lies. The more in tune you can be with your own life path, in all its originality, beauty and wonder, the more rewarding your life will be. The same is true for manifesting. Original, resourceful, intuitive and imaginative manifesting techniques - specifically created by you and for your goals - are the most potent way of manifesting positivity in your life.

My hope is that through manifesting positivity the world can be a better place for everyone. Share the benefits you manifest with the people in your life. The power of attraction is heightened when visualizing things for the good of all. If something works for you, share your wisdom. Remember that forgiveness, release and surrender are as vital to a life of manifesting as desire, and would make the world a much nicer place.

Value each step you take in reinventing your life. Be grateful for all the beauty in your life. Build upon the foundation of the life you have, and incorporate the best of what you know and the best of what you can imagine. Remember that crystal energy and universal energy are interconnected, so use your crystal connections wisely, with love and compassion, in all ways, for the good of all.

Crystal Clear

Choose crystals that resonate with you personally and they will have a profound impact on your life. Look around you and seek out the crystal friends who are already helping you. Get to know your crystals; allow space and time in your life to experience their support. Wear your jewellery with a new awareness. And remember, magic happens; if you are in need of a certain crystal, it will find its way to you.

Your crystals will help with your life path choices, enhance your decision-making skills, and illuminate your future. With their support, you will come to realize that challenges are opportunities to change your life, learn more, and love more deeply. Life can be busy, but it can also be fulfilling. Give yourself credit for your achievements. Respect yourself and make choices that move you into a place where you are happy, motivated and supported. An investment in you is so very important, so treat yourself with kindness.

Your crystals will promote your personal ascension process. They will help you access your inner wisdom and your connection with universal consciousness. They will help you deepen your understanding of your place in the Universe.

Positive feelings, thoughts, action, will and energy are now a part of your life. Every positive thought moves you into a better place for positive change to happen. When starting to manifest something new in your life, consider the following with an attitude of sincerity, love, happiness and gratitude:

What is it you want to manifest?
Be very clear in *thought*.

Does that fit with your life path?
Be honest with your *feelings*.

Which technique(s) will you use?
Choose *action* that resonates with who you are.

Which crystals best suit your needs?
Choose crystals that resonate strongly with your *will*.

What crystals do you have access to?
Commit *energy* to your plan.

When you obtain the positive change, how will you show *gratitude*?
Commit to thanksgiving.

The power you have to manifest is beautiful, strong and magnetic. You are an individual, creative and wise. Give yourself the opportunity to find your true potential; it is much more than you currently know. Your life path will become clearer as your self-awareness and confidence grow. Use manifesting techniques to help you move into a place of harmony with your wishes, goals and values. You are manifesting positivity in your life. Have confidence. *Live your enchanted life!*

Let crystals light your path clear.

Crystal Manifesting Qualities – Quick Reference Table

Purpose	Crystals that manifest and attract
Abundance	Alexandrite, Tourmaline, Jade
Angels	Celestite, Danburite
Anniversary	Ammolite, Diamond
Balance	Mangano Calcite, Amber
Blessing	Laguna Agate, Prehnite
Beauty	Aqua Aura, Pink Diamond, Rhodochrosite
Boundaries	Smoky Quartz, Chiastolite
Car	Tiger eye, Garnet
Career	Aventurine, Sapphire
Celebration	Yellow Tourmaline, Yellow Apatite
Change	Platinum, Red Jasper, Titanium
Charm	Larimar, Pearls
Children	Angelite, Peridot
Clarity	Lazulite, Vivianite
Commitment	Diamond, Yellow Gold
Communication	Turquoise, Dalmatian Stone, Tanzanite
Concentration	Malachite, Azurite, Amazonite
Connectivity	Limestone, Sardonyx
Coping with Death	Iolite, Black Marble, Jet, Lead Crystal
Creativity	Ruby in Zoisite, Chinese Writing Stone, Agate, Opal
Courage	Rainbow Obsidian, Indicolite, Bloodstone
Decision making	Zoisite, Leopard Skin Jasper
Destiny	Tanzanite, Geode
Divorce	Halite, Jet, Coloured Glass
Equality	Ametrine, Avalonite
Erase	Thunder Egg, Pewter
Endurance	Sandstone, Iron
Fairies	Lepidolite, Opal
Faith	Turquoise, Lithium Quartz, Gold
Fame	Emerald, Larimar
Family	Rhyolite, Pink Fluorite, Falcon Eye
Finances	Lapis Lazuli, Jade, Silver

Purpose	Crystals that manifest and attract
Forgiveness	Snowflake Obsidian, Bixbite
Friendship	Rhodochrosite, Moonstone
Fun	Strawberry, Siberian, Aqua Aura Quartz types
Generosity	Carnelian, Rhodochrosite
Gratitude	Pink Lace Agate, Howlite
Grief	Moonstone, Amber, Apache Tears
Growth	Green Fluorite, Amethyst, Rose Gold
Happiness	Gold Stone, Agate, Strawberry Quartz, Apatite
Health	Copper, Water Agate, Moss Agate, Fluorite
Home	Aegerine, Blue Lace Agate
Honesty	Tourmaline, Copper, Crazy Lace Agate
Hope	Shiva-Lingham, Rainbow Fluorite
Immortality	Emerald, Fossils
Inspiration	Purple Fluorite, Aquamarine
Learning	Unakite, Amazonite, Malachite
Life Path	Blue Lace Agate, Personal Crystal Astrology Crystals
Lost and Found	Lemurian Seed Crystals, Citrine
Love	Paraiba Tourmaline, Kunzite, Chrysoprase
Marriage	Morganite, Diamond, Sapphire, Ruby
Memory	Herkimer Diamond, Chalcopyrite
Manhood	Onyx, Jasper
Modifying Excesses	Kyanite, Blue Calcite
Money	Lapis Lazuli, Citrine, Yellow Sapphire, Serpentinite
Motivation	Hematite, Blue Topaz, Stainless Steel
New beginnings	Citrine, Moldavite, Labradorite
Optimism	Mookaite, Boji Stones
Originality	Olivine, Pietersite
Past Life Memory Recall	Tiger Eye, Calcite
Patience	Peace Agate, Danburite
Pets	Labradorite, Kyanite, Rose Quartz
Power	Rainbow Obsidian, Pyrite, Silver, Gold
Prayer	Sunstone, Violane, Celestite

Purpose	Crystals that manifest and attract
Pregnancy	Garnet, Bloodstone, Silver
Protection	Sapphire, Black Tourmaline, Tiger Eye
Purify	Clear Quartz, Diamond, Water
Recovery	Rhodonite, Tourmaline (all colours)
Reduce stress	All forms of Jasper and Calcite, Eudialyte
Reflection	Obsidian, Stainless Steel, Mirrors
Release	Aventurine, Chrysocolla
Relief	Spotted Lapis, Amber
Relationships	Kunzite, Chrysoprase, Gold
Romance	Ruby, Morganite
Safety	Red Calcite, Angelite
Security	Peridot, Falcon Eye
Soul Partner	Clear Crystals (e.g. Zircon, Diamond, Topaz, Glass)
Spirituality	Amethyst, Spinel
Success	Emerald, Diamond, Boji Stones, Rutilated Quartz
Transformation	Sodalite, Bronzite, Charoite
Transition	Iolite, Moldavite
Travel	Tektite, Elestial Quartz
Unconditional Love	Rose Quartz, Amegreen
Understanding	Fuchsite, Thulite, Selinite
Vocation	Magnetite, Slate, Shells, Glass
Weight (Healthy)	Blue Kyanite, Halite, Pewter
Womanhood	Agate, Amazonite
World Peace	Selenite, Clear Quartz, Peace Agate, White Marble

Warnings

Please seek professional medical advice from your doctor and other healthcare providers with regards to current medical conditions, genetic dispositions, diagnosis and treatment options, as this book is not in any way a substitute for medical advice.

Always supervise burning candles, particularly when children and pets are around. Take care that candles have a stable base so they can't tip over and ignite surrounding flammable material.

Essential oils should never be ingested. Some essential oils used in massage should be avoided while pregnant. If you are unsure if certain oils can be used safely, kindly consult your licensed alternative health practitioner for his or her advice and instruction.

Be aware that the following crystals should be used with care, and always wash your hands after touching them: Azurite, Boji-stones, Cerrusite, Chalcopyrite, Cinnabar, Diopside, Dioptase, Galena, Magnetite, Malachite, Meteorite, Molybdenum, Pyrite, Stibnite, Smithsonite and Sulphur. Do not mix the above crystals with water and consume.

Some crystals change colour when left in sunlight; for example, Ametrine, Celestite, Chrysoprase and Fluorite. Others crystals rust, such as iron-rich Meteorites. Others dissolve in water, such as Halite. Crystals that can be ruined in water include porous crystals such as Selenite, Angelite, Celestite and Gypsum.

Treat your crystals with respect. Keep them dust free and out of reach of small children. Over time crystals may crack or chip, and this is quite normal; remember crystals work just as well if they are cracked or faded.

Acknowledgements and Thanks

First and foremost, my deep love and gratitude to Ross and Harry.

Thank you to my mum Doris for her constant support. To my brother Ben and my dad Joe thank you for your support and love.

My heartfelt thanks go to:

Everyone at Earthdancer, in particular my publisher, Arwen Lentz, who is always both motivating and patient. (www.healingcrystalbooks.com)

Thierry Bogliolo and everyone at Findhorn Press for supporting me in my quest to publish.

Ella (Claudine) for her expertise and skill in the editing process.

Michael Gienger for his brilliant works.

Barry Jones (Director) from Brilliant Spheres Crystals, for permission to share with the world their range of amazingly powerful Crystal Candles™ (www.brilliantspherescrystals.com.au).

Radu Moisoiu (www.astrologyweekly.com) for his generosity and skill in creating and maintaining www.crystalastrology.com.

Huette and Julie Thomson at Awesome Universe (www.awesomeuniverse.com) for their constant support and friendship.

Kellie the Crystal Deva of Avalon Crystals™ (www.neatstuff.net/avalon) for her generosity.

Extra special thanks and blessings go to Ruth, Jean, Mary, Anita, Catherine, Jeanine, Joanne, Rosemary, Heather, Barbara, Steve, Sean, Danuta, Mark, Alyssa, James, Judith, Marilyn, Luke, Jack, Rob, Lisa and all my friends – you help crystallize my life.

Sources

Picture Credits
Picture p. 44-45: © Elena Yakusheva/Shutterstock

Favourite Online Crystal Shops and Websites
Avalon Crystals: www.neatstuff.net/avalon
Awesome Universe: www.awesomeuniverse.com
Healing Crystal Books: www.healingcrystalbooks.com
Astrology Weekly: www.astrologyweekly.com
Crystal Astrology: www.crystalastrology.com
Findhorn Press: www.findhornpress.com
Soul Indulgence: www.soulindulgence.com.au

Suggested Reading

Costelloe, Marina. *The Complete Guide to Crystal Astrology: 360 Crystals and Sabian Symbols for Personal Health, Astrology and Numerology*, Earthdancer a Findhorn Press Imprint, 2007.

Cunningham, Scott. *Cunningham's Encyclopedia of Crystal, Gem & Metal Magic*, Minnesota, Llewellyn Publications, 2002.

Gienger, Michael. *Healing Crystals, The A-Z Guide to 430 Gemstones*, Earthdancer a Findhorn Press Imprint, 2005.

Gienger, Michael. *Purifying Crystals: The Cleansing, Recharging, Care and Protection, by and for Your Crystals,* Earthdancer a Findhorn Press Imprint, 2008.

Goebel, Joachim and Gienger, Michael. *Gem Water: How to Prepare and Use Over 130 Crystal Waters for Therapeutic Treatments*, Earthdancer a Findhorn Press Imprint, 2008.

Melody. *Love is in the Earth, a Kaleidoscope of Crystals*, Wheat Ridge, Colorado, Earth-Love Publishing, 1995.

Silveira, Isabel. *Quartz Crystals: A Guide to Identifying Quartz Crystals and Their Healing Properties,* Earthdancer a Findhorn Press Imprint, 2008.

Notes

[1] Isabel Silveira, *Quartz Crystals*, Earthdancer a Findhorn Press Imprint, 2008 (p.48).

[2] Michael Gienger, *Purifying Crystals: How to clear, charge and purify your healing crystals*, Earthdancer a Findhorn Press Imprint, 2008.

[3] *Gem Water: How to Prepare and Use Over 130 Crystal Waters for Therapeutic Treatments*, Earthdancer a Findhorn Press Imprint, 2008.

[4] Michael Gienger, *Crystal Massage for Health and Healing*, Earthdancer a Findhorn Press Imprint, 2006.

***

Edition Cairn Elen

"After Elen had accomplished her wandering through the world, she placed a Cairn at the end of the Sarn Elen. Her path then led her back to the land between evening and morning. From this Cairn originated all stones that direct the way at crossroads up until today."*

(From a Celtic myth)

'Cairn Elen'** is the term used in Gaelic-speaking areas to refer to the ancient slab stones on track ways. They mark the spiritual paths, both the paths of the earth and that of knowledge.

These paths are increasingly falling into oblivion. Just as the old paths of the earth disappear under the modern asphalt streets, so also does certain ancient wisdom disappear under the data flood of modern information. For this reason, the desire and aim of the Edition Cairn Elen is to preserve ancient wisdom and link it with modern knowledge – for a flourishing future!

The Edition Cairn Elen in Neue Erde Verlag is published by Michael Gienger. The objective of the Edition is to present knowledge from research and tradition that has remained unpublished up until now. Areas of focus are nature, naturopathy and health, as well as consciousness and spiritual freedom.

Apart from current specialised literature, stories, fairytales, novels, lyric and artistic publications will also be published within the scope of Edition Cairn Elen. The knowledge thus transmitted reaches out not only to the intellect bu' also to the heart.

Contact
Edition Cairn Elen, Anja & Michael Gienger, Fürststraße 13, 72072 Tübingen
Tel: +49 (0) 7071 36 47 20, Fax: +49 (0) 7071 38 868,
eMail: buecher@michael-gienger.de, www.michael-gienger.de

---

[1] Celtic 'cairn' [pronounced: carn] = 'Stone' (usually placed as an intentional shaped heap of stones), 'sarn' = 'Path', 'Elen, Helen' = 'Goddess of the Roads'

** Cairn Elen: in ancient and contemporary British culture, cairns are generally thought to be intentionally hea ed piles of stones, rather than an individual stone such as a boulder or standing stone.

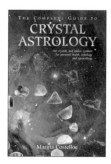

Marina Costelloe
The Complete Guide to Crystal Astrology
360 crystals and sabian symbols for personal health,
astrology and numerology
Paperback, full colour throughout, 224 pages, with 360 pictures,
ISBN 978-1-84409-103-4

Using this guide the reader will discover which of the 360 crystal elements is associated with the position of the sun at the time of their birth; learn about the relationship between birth charts, crystals, and planets; and find out how personal crystal elements are connected to numerology. The books also explores Marc Edmund Jones key words, Sabian symbols, and Jane Ridder-Patrick healing body points, ultimately teaching the readers how to reach a higher life potential.

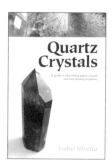

Isabel Silveira
Quartz Crystals
A guide to identifying quartz crystals and their healing properties
Paperback, full colour throughout, 80 pages,
ISBN 978-1-84409-148-5

This visually impressive book brings the reader up close to the beauty and diversity of the quartz crystal family. Its unique and concise presentation allows the reader to quickly and easily identify an array of quartz crystals and become familiar with their distinctive features and energetic properties.

Michael Gienger
The Healing Crystal First Aid Manual
A practical A to Z of common ailments and illnesses and
how they can be best treated with crystal therapy
288 pages, with 16 colour plates, ISBN 978-1-84409-084-6

This is an easy-to-use A-Z guide for treating many common ailments and illnesses with the help of crystal therapy. It includes a comprehensive colour appendix with photographs and short descriptions of each gemstone recommended.

Michael Gienger
Healing Crystals
The A - Z Guide to 430 Gemstones
Paperback, full colour throughout, 96 pages, ISBN 978-1-84409-067-9

All the important information about 430 healing gemstones in a neat pocket-book! Michael Gienger, known for his popular introductory work 'Crystal Power, Crystal Healing', here presents a comprehensive directory of all the gemstones currently in use. In a clear, concise and precise style, with pictures accompanying the text, the author describes the characteristics and healing functions of each crystal.

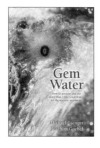

Michael Gienger, Joachim Goebel
Gem Water
How to prepare and use more than 130 crystal waters
for therapeutic treatments
Paperback, full colour throughout, 96 pages, ISBN 978-1-84409-131-7

Adding crystals to water is both visually appealing and healthy. It is a known fact that water carries mineral information and Gem Water provides effective remedies, acting quickly on a physical level. It is similar and complementary to wearing crystals, but the effects are not necessarily the same.

Gem Water needs to be prepared and applied with care; this book explains everything you need to know to get started!

Michael Gienger
Purifying Crystals
How to clear, charge and purify your healing crystals
Paperback, full colour throughout, 64 pages, ISBN 978-1-84409-147-8

Correct cleansing of crystals is an essential prerequisite for working with them successfully. But how can this be done effectively? There appear to be many different opinions on the subject. This useful little guidebook provides information about the known and less known methods for cleansing crystals, clearly illustrating which method is best for which aim, whether it be discharging, charging, cleansing on the outer level, cleansing on the energetic level, or elimination of attached information. Also included are step-by-step instructions for performing a crystal cleansing ceremony, and information about how to clear, cleanse and protect rooms with the help of crystals.

Michael Gienger
Crystal Massage for Health and Healing
Paperback, full colour throughout, 112 pages, ISBN 978-1-84409-077-8

This book introduces a spectrum of massage possibilities using healing crystals. The techniques have been developed and refined by experts, and this wisdom is conveyed in simple and direct language, enhanced by photos. Any interested amateur will be amazed at the wealth of new therapeutic possibilities that open up when employing the healing power of crystals.

Monika Grundmann
Crystal Balance
A step-by-step guide to beauty and health through crystal massage
Paperback, full colour throughout, 112 pages,
ISBN 978-1-84409-132-4

Our physical wellbeing reflects every aspect of our lives and inner selves. As a result, massage is able to influence us on every level – mind, body and spirit.

The Crystal Balance method aims to help our bodies relax and recover, encouraging our soul and spirit to 'bethemselves'. When we are truly 'ourselves', we are beautiful. It is as simple as that.

Ewald Kliegel
Crystal Wands
For healing, massage therapy and reflexology
Paperback, full colour throughout, 144 pages, ISBN 978-1-84409-152-2

What could you achieve with a crystal wand? How can you find out which crystal wand best suits your needs? How can you perform a relaxing massage combining crystal wands and reflexology? These are just a few of the questions answered in this practical guidebook. Learn to use crystal wands for reflexology, for massage, to trace meridian lines or to balance the chakras; whatever your therapeutic aim, these beautiful energetic tools can help you. Basic information on reflexology, crystal healing and testing methods is also included, as well as full massage programs for your immediate use.

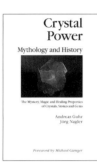

Andreas Guhr, Jörg Nagler
Crystal Power, Mythology and History
160 pages, full colour throughout, ISBN 978-1-84409-085-3

This book reveals the long- standing significance, high regard and use in therapy and healing of stones, crystals and gems – from the earliest civilizations such as Mesopotamia and Ancient Egypt, throughthe classical world of Greece and Rome and into medieval European cultures. In addition, there is acomprehensive Appendix, in which minerals and crystals are listed with their respective mineralogical,historical, astrological and healing properties.

Fred Hageneder, Anne Heng
The Tree Angel Oracle
36 colour cards (95 x 133 mm) plus book, 112 pages,
ISBN 978-1-84409-078-5

There are two types of angels: those with wings, and those with leaves. For thousands of years, those seeking advice or wanting to give thanks to Mother Nature have walked the ancient paths into the sacred grove. Because today sacred groves have become scarcer, and venerable old trees in tranquil spots are hard to find when we need them, Earthdancer is pleased to present this tree oracle to bring the tree angels closer to us all once more.

Satya Singh and Fred Hageneder
Tree Yoga: A Workbook
Strengthen Your Personal Yoga Practice
Through the Living Wisdom of Trees
Paperback, two colours, 224 pages, ISBN 978-1-84409-119-5

Revealing the dynamic bond between man and tree, this inspired yoga handbook offers a detailed review of the ancient wisdom of Kundalini Yoga and unveils the inner power of trees, as well as their unique characteristics and energies. Yoga exercises based on this wisdom are provided, each of which operates by fostering a connection with the inner essence of a different tree, from birch and lime to elm and rowan. With full illustrations and step-by-step instructions.

EARTHDANCER A FINDHORN PRESS IMPRINT
For further information and book catalogue contact:
Findhorn Press, 305a The Park, Forres, IV36 3TE, Scotland.
Earthdancer Books is an imprint of Findhorn Press.
tel +44 (0)1309-690582, fax +44 (0)131 777 2711
info@findhornpress.com, www.earthdancer.co.uk, www.findhornpress.com
For more information on crystal healing visit www.crystalhealingbooks.com

EARTHDANCER

A FINDHORN PRESS IMPRINT